Petra Lihocky

# Klett
# Grammatik im Griff
# Englisch 5./6. Klasse

Mein Übungsbuch für
Gymnasium und Realschule

Klett Lerntraining

Petra Lihocky ist Gymnasiallehrerin für die Fächer Englisch und Deutsch.

**Hinweis:**
Zu diesem Buch gehören Online-Tests unter
www.klasse5bis10.klett-lerntraining.de.
Der Zugang zu den Online-Abschlusstests ist bis drei Jahre nach Ersterscheinen des Buches gewährleistet.

Bibliografische Information der Deutschen Nationalbibliothek
Die Deutsche Nationalbibliothek verzeichnet diese Publikation in der Deutschen Nationalbibliografie; detaillierte bibliografische Daten sind im Internet über http://dnb.dnb.de abrufbar.



1. Auflage 2018


www.klett-lerntraining.de
Umschlaggestaltung: Sabine Kaufmann, Stuttgart
Umschlagfoto: istockfoto (Viorika), Calgary, Alberta
Außenredaktion: Sabine Schlimm, Hamburg
Satz: DTP-Studio Andrea Eckhardt, Göppingen
Druck: medienhaus Plump GmbH, Rheinbreitbach
Printed in Germany
ISBN 978-3-12-927409-5

# Inhaltsverzeichnis

## So übst du mit diesem Buch

Liebe Schülerin, lieber Schüler,

du möchtest fit in der englischen Grammatik werden?
Dann ist „Grammatik im Griff Englisch" genau das richtige Übungsbuch für dich! Es hilft dir dabei, alle **wichtigen Themen** der englischen Grammatik zu wiederholen und zu üben. Gehe so vor:

**Schritt 1**

**Suche** aus dem Inhaltsverzeichnis das **Thema heraus**, dass du wiederholen möchtest.

**Schritt 2**

**Lies** das **Merkwissen** im Kasten **durch**. Dort steht alles, was du zu diesem Thema wissen und können solltest.

**Schritt 3**

Jetzt kannst du mit den vielen unterschiedlichen **Aufgaben üben**. Einige Aufgaben lassen sich aus Platzgründen nicht im Buch lösen – lege dir dafür ein Heft zu.

**Schritt 4**

**Vergleiche** deine Antworten mit den **Lösungen** hinten im Buch.

**Schritt 5**

Wenn du ein Kapitel abgeschlossen hast, kannst du dich mit dem **Abschlusstest online testen**. Die Ergebnisse aus dem Test kannst du in die Tabelle am Kapitelende übertragen. So behältst du immer den Überblick.

## So funktioniert der Abschlusstest online

Gehe auf **https://www.klett-lerntraining.de/9Y2A**.

Du erhältst eine Übersicht über alle Kapitel und darunter alle verfügbaren Abschlusstests.
Wähle einen passenden Test aus und bearbeite die Aufgaben.

Du kannst alle Online-Tests mit und ohne Anmeldung nutzen.
**Bitte beachte:** Wenn du dich nicht anmeldest, kann dein Lernstand in den Tests **nicht gespeichert** werden.

Eine Anmeldung ist nur möglich, wenn du dich vorher bei uns registriert hast. Dafür musst du dir einen Benutzernamen und ein Passwort ausdenken und deine E-Mail-Adresse angeben. Dann erhältst du einen Aktivierungslink per E-Mail.

Informationen zu Registrierung und Anmeldung findest du immer unter „**Hilfe**" in unserem Lernportal www.klasse5bis10.klett-lerntraining.de.

Viel Erfolg wünschen dir die Autoren und das Team von Klett-Lerntraining

# 1 Artikel und Nomen

## 1.1 Der unbestimmte Artikel

### Die Formen des unbestimmten Artikels

Dem unbestimmten Artikel **ein** oder **eine** (z. B. in „ein Mann", „eine Maus") entspricht im Englischen das Wort ***a*** bzw. ***an***. Welche Form du verwenden musst, hängt allein von der Aussprache des folgenden Wortes ab:

| ***a*** vor Konsonanten (Mitlauten) | ***an*** vor Vokalen (Selbstlauten: a, e, i, o, u) |
|---|---|
| **a** pupil<br>**a** tiny mouse<br>**a** nice girl<br>! **a** unit | **an** apple<br>**an** uncle<br>**an** open book |

**Achtung**:
Häufig wird der Buchstabe **u** als [ju] ausgesprochen, wie in *unit*, *use* oder *uniform*. Vor solchen Wörtern musst du ebenfalls ***a*** verwenden!

### Die Verwendung des unbestimmten Artikels

- Der unbestimmte Artikel (*indefinite article*) bezieht sich auf Nomen im Singular, d. h. einzelne Personen, Tiere oder Dinge.
- Anders als im Deutschen musst du im Englischen den unbestimmten Artikel auch vor Berufsbezeichnungen verwenden:

| Mein Vater ist Lehrer. | My father is **a** teacher. |
|---|---|
| Sie ist Taxifahrerin. | She is **a** taxi driver. |

## Aufgabe 1: The Singasongs

**Lies den Text über Suzy Singasong und ihre musikalische Familie. Unterstreiche alle unbestimmten Artikel und die dazugehörigen Nomen und schreibe sie in die Liste.**

In the picture you can see a family. There is a girl with a saxophone. This is Suzy Singasong. You can also see a woman. She is Suzy's mother. She is singing. On the left there is a boy. This is Tim, Suzy's brother. He is playing the drums. There is also a man with a guitar. He is Suzy's father. On the floor there is a cat. This is Lily.

a) a family b) ____________________

c) ____________________ d) ____________________

e) ____________________ f) ____________________

g) ____________________ h) ____________________

## Aufgabe 2: An English family

**Verwende nun noch einmal die Wörterliste aus Aufgabe 1 und kombiniere sie mit den folgenden Adjektiven. Achte darauf, ob du *a* oder *an* benutzen musst.**

a) English – *an English family*
b) young – ________________
c) new – ________________
d) interesting – ________________
e) tall – ________________
f) cool – ________________
g) old – ________________
h) small – ________________

## Aufgabe 3: Jobs, jobs, jobs

**In den Wörterschlangen sind acht Berufsbezeichnungen versteckt. Finde sie und ergänze sie zusammen mit dem unbestimmten Artikel.**

ahgrteachertefkshopassistantrgzumanagergpuzactorvthg

busdrivermrereporterewrscaretakerorpucookwvio

a) She drives a bus: She is ______________________________.

b) He plays in films: He is ______________________________.

c) She sells clothes: She is ______________________________.

d) He looks after houses: He is ______________________________.

e) She makes pizza: She is ______________________________.

f) He works for a newspaper: He is ______________________________.

g) She is the boss of the shop: She is ______________________________.

h) He works at school: He is ______________________________.

## Aufgabe 4: A picnic

**Hier siehst du, was Familie Singasong zu ihrem Picknick mitnimmt. Schreibe die englische Bezeichnung zusammen mit dem unbestimmten Artikel unter die einzelnen Bilder.**

a) *a banana*  b) ____________  c) ____________

d) ____________  e) ____________  f) ____________

## Aufgabe 5: Awful food

**Es gibt auch Dinge, die man lieber nicht zu einem Picknick mitnehmen möchte ... Kombiniere die Adjektive unten mit den Lebensmitteln aus Aufgabe 4.**

a) bad – *a bad banana*  b) sour – ____________

c) tiny – ____________  d) old – ____________

e) bitter – ____________  f) dry – ____________

## 1.2 Der bestimmte Artikel

### Die Form des bestimmten Artikels

Dem bestimmten Artikel **der**, **die** oder **das** entspricht im Englischen das Wort ***the***. Der bestimmte Artikel (*definite article*) hat im Englischen nur eine einzige Form. Es gibt allerdings zwei verschiedene Arten, ihn auszusprechen. Wie beim unbestimmten Artikel ist entscheidend, mit welchem Laut das folgende Wort anfängt:

| [ðə] vor Konsonanten (Mitlauten) | [ði] vor Vokalen (Selbstlauten: a, e, i, o, u) |
|---|---|
| **the** [ðə] pupil | **the** [ði] apple |
| **the** [ðə] tiny mouse | **the** [ði] uncle |
| ! **the** [ðə] unit | **the** [ði] open book |

### Die Verwendung des bestimmten Artikels

- ***The*** steht vor Nomen im Singular und im Plural. Es bezieht sich auf (näher) bestimmte Personen, Tiere oder Dinge:

  Look at **the** cat over there!
  **The** pen on the table is red.
  **The** boys and girls in my tutor group are very nice.

- Vor Eigennamen steht kein bestimmter Artikel. Anders als im Deutschen gilt das auch für Straßennamen:

  Mr Smith wants to go to London.
  Mike lives in Chester Road.

- Merke dir folgende vom Deutschen abweichende Wendungen:

| | |
|---|---|
| mit **dem Rad/Bus/Zug** etc. fahren | to go by bike/bus/train |
| Klavier/Gitarre/Schlagzeug etc. spielen | to play **the** piano/**the** guitar/ **the** drums |

- Achte auf die Besonderheit bei Wörtern wie school/church/university:

| Bezug auf eine **Aktivität**: kein Artikel | Bezug auf das **Gebäude**: bestimmter Artikel |
|---|---|
| Ben is **at school**. | We can meet **in front of the school**. |
| Ben ist in der Schule (d.h. im Unterricht). | Wir können uns vor der Schule treffen (d.h. vor dem Gebäude). |

## Aufgabe 6: What Tim needs for school

**Diese Dinge darf Tim morgens nicht vergessen. Kreuze jeweils an, wie der bestimmte Artikel ausgesprochen wird.**

| | [ðə] | [ði] |
|---|---|---|
| a) the uniform | ☐ | ☐ |
| b) the exercise books | ☐ | ☐ |
| c) the new pencils | ☐ | ☐ |
| d) the old ruler | ☐ | ☐ |
| e) the school bag | ☐ | ☐ |
| f) the tiny rubber | ☐ | ☐ |
| g) the big pencil-case | ☐ | ☐ |
| h) the important mobile | ☐ | ☐ |
| i) the tasty sandwiches | ☐ | ☐ |
| j) the expensive sports shoes | ☐ | ☐ |

## Aufgabe 7: Suzy's school

**In dieser Aufgabe erfährst du etwas über Suzys Schulalltag. Entscheide bei jeder Lücke: Brauchst du den bestimmten Artikel oder gar keinen Artikel?**

a) Suzy needs ______ alarm clock next to ______ bed to wake up every morning.

b) Then she puts on ______ uniform of her school.

c) ______ school uniforms are very important in England.

d) ______ uniform of Suzy's school is red.

e) Suzy likes ______ colour red.

f) But she doesn't like ______ woollen (*aus Wolle*) skirt of her uniform.

g) Suzy hates ______ wool.

h) Suzy's school is in ______ Einstein Road.

i) She usually goes there by ______ bus.

j) She meets all her friends at ______ school.

k) In the morning, she waits in front of ______ school for them.

l) She often talks to them about ______ boys in their tutor group.

m) Suzy spends a lot of time at ______ school.

n) Sometimes she goes to ______ park behind ______ school.

o) Then she plays ______ saxophone there.

## Aufgabe 8: Tim's room

**Tim erzählt dir etwas über sein Zimmer. Entscheide bei jeder Lücke, ob du den unbestimmten Artikel, den bestimmten Artikel oder gar keinen Artikel einsetzen musst.**

a) I have got ______ big room of my own.

b) In ______ room I can play ______ drums.

c) There are ______ posters on ______ walls.

d) On ______ posters you can see ______ famous drummers.

e) I have only ______ small wardrobe in my room.

f) ______ wardrobe isn't big enough for all my stuff.

g) So usually a lot of my clothes are on ______ floor.

h) I am not ______ very tidy (*ordentlich*) person.

i) In my room there is also ______ old desk.

j) ______ desk is ______ present from my grandfather.

k) All the things for ______ school are in ______ desk.

l) There are a lot of books on ______ shelf in ______ corner (*Ecke*).

m) ______ books are about ______ computers and ______ sports.

n) Behind ______ door there is ______ pile (*Stapel*) of music magazines.

o) ______ best music magazine comes from ______ Manchester.

## 1.3 Pluralformen der Nomen

### Regelmäßige Bildung des Plurals

Du bildest den Plural der meisten englischen Nomen, indem du direkt an die Singularform ein **s** anhängst:

| **Singular** | **Plural** |
|---|---|
| ball | ball**s** |
| game | game**s** |

Nach Zischlauten [s, z, ʃ, tʃ, ʒ, dʒ] hängst du zur Pluralbildung **es** an.
Aber: Nach Zischlaut + **e** hängst du zur Plurabildung nur **s** an.

| **Singular** | **Plural** |
|---|---|
| bus | bus**es** |
| exerci**se** | exercise**s** |

### Unregelmäßige Pluralformen

- Nomen mit der Endung **-f(e)** bilden den Plural meist mit -**ves**:

| Singular | Plural |
|---|---|
| knife | kni**ves** |
| thief | thie**ves** |

- Nomen mit der Endung Konsonant **+ y** bilden den Plural mit -**ies**, Nomen mit der Endung Vokal **+ y** bilden den Plural mit **s**:

| Singular | Plural |
|---|---|
| baby | bab**ies** |
| boy | boy**s** |

- Einzelne Wörter bilden den Plural unregelmäßig. Diese Formen musst du lernen. Beispiele hierfür sind:

| **Singular** | **Plural** |
|---|---|
| man | men |
| woman | women |
| mouse | mice |

## Aufgabe 9: Counting animals

**Schreibe unter jedes Bild, wie viele Tiere abgebildet sind.**

a) *two cows*

b) ____________________
____________________

c) ____________________
____________________

d) ____________________
____________________

e) ____________________
____________________

f) ____________________
____________________

## Aufgabe 10: Parts of the body

**Notiere die Bezeichnung für das jeweilige Körperteil mit dem unbestimmten Artikel. Bilde dann von allen Wörtern die Pluralform.**

| | | |
|---|---|---|
| a) | *a face* | *faces* |
| b) | | |
| c) | | |
| d) | | |
| e) | | |
| f) | | |
| g) | | |
| h) | | |
| i) | | |
| j) | | |

## Aufgabe 11: Our furniture

**Trage den Plural der Wörter ein.**

a) table ______________ b) chair ______________

c) sofa ______________ d) cupboard ______________

e) picture ______________ f) bed ______________

g) shelf ______________ h) desk ______________

## Aufgabe 12: At the circus

**Ergänze die angegebenen Wörter in den Lücken. Setze sie dazu – falls nötig – in den Plural.**

**show – girl – woman – family – boy – tiger – clown – acrobat – parrot (*Papagei*) – circus – man**

a) Suzy, Tim and their parents go to the ______________ today.

b) There are many other ______________ like the Singasongs there.

c) Tim wants to see the three white ______________.

d) Suzy is waiting for the ______________ with the red nose.

e) Finally the ______________ begins.

f) Mrs Singasong loves the two speaking ______________.

g) Mr Singasong likes the group of Chinese ______________.

h) In the end, everybody in the audience (*Publikum*) is happy:

______________ and ______________,

______________ and ______________.

## 1.4 *S*-Genitiv und *of*-Genitiv

### Der *s*-Genitiv

Der Genitiv drückt aus, wem etwas gehört oder zugeordnet ist. Den ***s*-Genitiv** (*s-genitive*) verwendest du meist bei **Personen** und **Tieren**. Du bildest ihn so:

| | | |
|---|---|---|
| Singular | Apostroph **+ s** | Kate**'s** sister<br>my Mum**'s** car |
| Regelmäßiger Plural | Apostroph | the boys' football<br>the dogs' basket |
| Unregelmäßiger Plural | Apostroph **+ s** | the women**'s** mobiles<br>people**'s** lives |

**Achte darauf, die folgenden Formen nicht miteinander zu verwechseln:**

| ***s*-Genitiv** | **Andere Formen** |
|---|---|
| **The girl's** bike is red. | **The girls** are here. (Plural) |
| **Mike's** dog is old. | **Mike's** got a dog. (Kurzform von *has*) |
| **Mia's** friend is nice. | **Mia's** my friend. (Kurzform von *is*) |

### Der *of*-Genitiv

Den ***of*-Genitiv** (*of-genitive*) verwendest du in der Regel bei **Dingen**:
the windows **of** the house — the first day **of** the week

**Mengenangaben** werden im Englischen ebenfalls mit **of** gebildet:
two bottles **of** water — a cup **of** tea

## Aufgabe 13: Who owns what?

**Bilde den *s*-Genitiv und ergänze bei Bedarf den bestimmten Artikel.**

Beispiel: a) *Suzy's saxophone*

a) Suzy/saxophone
b) Tim/drums
c) family/house
d) parents/room
e) Dad/guitar
f) Mum/clothes
g) Lily/milk
h) neighbours/car
i) friends/dog
j) uncle/watch
k) teacher/pen
l) pupils/uniforms

## Aufgabe 14: A birthday party for Mr Singasong

**Tim und Suzy bereiten für ihren Vater eine Überraschungsfeier vor. Dazu schreiben sie auf, was sie brauchen. Verbinde die Nomen mit dem Genitiv. Überlege dabei: *s*-Genitiv oder *of*-Genitiv?**

Beispiel: a) candles/a box – *a box of candles*

b) list/the guests ______________________
c) the children/ideas ______________________
d) a big bag/decoration ______________________
e) Dad/address book ______________________
f) the relatives/phone numbers ______________________
g) Mum/help ______________________
h) funny games/a book ______________________
i) the living room/the keys ______________________
j) the birthday song/the melody ______________________

## Aufgabe 15: Preparing the birthday party

**Sieh dir die hervorgehobenen Wörter an und kreuze an, um welche Form es sich dabei handelt.**

| | s-Genitiv Singular | s-Genitiv Plural | Einfaches Plural-s | Kurzform von *has* | Kurzform von *is* |
|---|---|---|---|---|---|
| a) Tim: "**Dad's** work finishes at 5 pm." | | | | | |
| b) Suzy: "So **he's** got free time after that." | | | | | |
| c) Tim: "Okay, then the party starts at 6. **That's** a good idea." | | | | | |
| d) Suzy: "**Everything's** ready for the party?" | | | | | |
| e) Tim: "No, we still need to buy some **things**." | | | | | |
| f) Suzy: "Do you think we can take our **parents'** purse for the shopping?" | | | | | |
| g) Tim: "No, I think we need **Mum's** okay to take the money." | | | | | |

## Aufgabe 16: The birthday cake

**Suzy und Tim kaufen die Zutaten für Mr Singasongs Geburtstagskuchen ein. Schreibe die Einkaufsliste. Bedenke, dass die beiden ganze Packungen kaufen müssen! Die Mengenangaben können dir helfen.**

**a bottle – a bar – a tin – a bag – a packet – a box – a pound – a glass**

Beispiel: a) *a pound of butter*

List of ingredients (*Zutatenliste*):
500 g butter, 6 eggs, 300 g flour, 250 g sugar, 500 ml milk, 50 g carrots, 100 g chocolate, 50 g hazelnuts, 50 g coconut flakes (*Kokosflocken*), 50 g honey, 5 candles, some tinned peaches (*Pfirsiche in der Dose*)

# Abschlusstest online 1

Super! Du hast das **Kapitel 1 – Artikel und Nomen** durchgearbeitet. Du hast gelernt, wann du welchen Artikel vor ein Substantiv setzt, wie der Plural gebildet wird und wie du mit den verschiedenen Genitivformen ausdrückst, was jemandem gehört oder etwas zugeordnet wird.

**So funktioniert der Abschlusstest online:**
Um deinen Lernerfolg zu überprüfen, kannst du nun die Abschlusstests machen. Gehe auf
**https://www.klett-lerntraining.de/9Y2A**
und wähle das Kapitel und einen Test aus.

Welche Tests es gibt, siehst du unten in der Tabelle. Nach jedem Test bekommst du eine Auswertung.

Willst du immer im Blick haben, welche Themen du schon kannst oder was du besser wiederholen solltest? Dann schreibe deine Ergebnisse in die Tabelle.

## Mein Ergebnis im Abschlusstest online – Kapitel 1

| Thema | Mein Ergebnis |
|---|---|
| Bestimmter und unbestimmter Artikel | |
| Pluralformen der Nomen | |
| *s*-Genitiv und *of*-Genitiv | |

# 2 Pronomen und Begleiter

## 2.1 Subjekt- und Objektform der Personalpronomen

### Die Formen der Personalpronomen

Personalpronomen (*personal pronouns*) stehen für ein Substantiv (Nomen), d. h. für Personen, Tiere oder auch Gegenstände.
Das Personalpronomen kann im Satz **Subjekt** oder **Objekt** sein.

Look, there is Mr Harris. **He** is my teacher. (**He**: Subjekt)
Yes, I know **him**. (**him**: Objekt)

Die Formen der Personalpronomen lauten:

| | **Subjektform** | | **Objektform** | |
|---|---|---|---|---|
| Singular | **I** | ich | **me** | mir/mich |
| | **you** | du/Sie | **you** | dir/dich/Ihnen/Sie |
| | **he** | er | **him** | ihm/ihn |
| | **she** | sie | **her** | sie |
| | **it** | es | **it** | es |
| Plural | **we** | wir | **us** | uns |
| | **you** | ihr/Sie | **you** | euch/Ihnen/Sie |
| | **they** | sie | **them** | ihnen/sie |

### Verwendung der Personalpronomen

- *I* schreibst du immer groß (nicht nur am Satzanfang).
- *He* steht für eine männliche Person, *she* steht für eine weibliche Person (niemals für eine Sache!).
- Für Tiere steht *it*, es sei denn, du kennst ihren Namen, der eindeutig weiblich oder männlich ist. Dann verwendest du *he* oder *she*.
- Dinge werden im Englischen immer mit *it* bezeichnet.

### Besonderheiten der Objektform

Im Englischen haben die Personalpronomen jeweils nur eine Objektform. Die englische Form ***me*** kann daher **mir** oder **mich** bedeuten:

| | |
|---|---|
| She shows **me** the book. | Sie zeigt **mir** das Buch. |
| Tim doesn't find **me**. | Tim findet **mich** nicht. |

Auch nach Präpositionen steht im Englischen die Objektform des Personalpronomens:

She wants to talk to **me**.
They want to play with **him**.

## Aufgabe 1: Suzy Singasong is talking about her family

**Lies dir durch, was Suzy erzählt, und unterstreiche alle Personalpronomen.**

Hi, I'm Suzy Singasong. Do you like music? Then come and meet my family. We all play together in a band. It's called "The Singasong Family". My brother Tim practices the drums for hours every day. He often gets on my nerves (*geht mir auf die Nerven*). But my parents are really nice. They aren't very strict (*streng*). I love our cat Lily. Sometimes she listens to our music, too. We have only got one problem: our neighbours. They don't like the noise we make.

## Aufgabe 2: An interview with Suzy

**Suzy beantwortet einige Fragen über sich und ihre Familie für die Schülerzeitung. Verwende Personalpronomen für ihre Antworten.**

a) "How old are you?" "_________'m twelve."

b) "Where are you and your family from?" "_________'re from London."

c) "What are your parents like?" "_________'re cool."

d) "What's your favourite sport?" "_________'s swimming."

e) "How old is your brother?" "_________'s fifteen."

f) "What's your mother's job?" "_________'s a taxi driver."

g) "What's your father's job?" "_________'s a teacher."

h) "What are your teachers like?" "_________'re nice."

## Aufgabe 3: A garden party at the Singasongs' house

**Für die Gartenparty heute Abend muss viel vorbereitet werden. Suzys und Tims Mutter hat daher viele Aufträge für die beiden. Setze passende Personalpronomen in der Objektform in die Lücken ein.**

a) Your dad is in the kitchen. Can you help _________ with the sandwiches?

b) Here are the glasses. Put _________ on the table, please.

c) Aunt Helen doesn't know about the party yet. Please phone _________.

d) I need another plate. Bring _________ that one over there, please!

e) Grandma is already at the bus station. Can you pick _________ up there?

f) The cake for the party is ready. Get _________ at the baker's, please.

g) Tim, we want to put the table in the garden. Can you help _________?

h) Where are all our CDs, Suzy? Tell _________, please.

## Aufgabe 4: At school

**Auch in der Schule bekommen Suzy und Tim jeden Tag viele Anweisungen von ihren Lehrern. Schreibe die Sätze richtig auf.**

a) the lesson/start/us/let/now

b) me/about/tell/your homework

c) say/you/again/could/it/please?

d) can/you/the game/with/play/them

e) next week/me/show/your pictures

f) ask/the exercise/her/about

g) him/help/the grammar/with/please

h) can/talk/you/about/with your neighbours/it

## Aufgabe 5: A morning with the Singasongs

**Hier erfährst du, was an einem typischen Morgen bei Familie Singasong geschieht. Schreibe die Sätze auf, indem du die unterstrichenen Ausdrücke durch Personalpronomen ersetzt.**

a) <u>Tim</u> hears <u>the ringing of the alarm clock</u>.

b) <u>Suzy</u> dreams about <u>the next holidays</u>.

c) <u>Tim</u> can't find <u>his clothes</u>.

d) <u>Mrs Singasong</u> calls <u>her children</u>.

e) <u>Mr Singasong</u> tells <u>jokes</u>.

f) <u>Suzy</u> plays a trick on <u>Tim</u>.

g) <u>Suzy and Tim</u> eat <u>their breakfast</u>.

h) <u>Suzy</u> looks for <u>her schoolbag</u>.

i) <u>Lily the cat</u> catches <u>a mouse</u>.

j) <u>Suzy's father</u> kisses <u>his wife</u>.

## 2.2 Die Possessivbegleiter

Begleiter bestimmen Substantive näher. Possessivbegleiter (*possessive determiners*) drücken aus, wem oder zu wem etwas gehört. Ihre Formen lauten:

| | | |
|---|---|---|
| Singular | **my** | Hi, I am Kelly and this is **my** sister. |
| | **your** | You must come tonight. Bring **your** dog, too. |
| | **his** | He is my best friend. I like **his** smile. |
| | **her** | She is ten and **her** brother is twelve. |
| | **its** | This is a big apple. **Its** colour is red. |
| Plural | **our** | We live in London. **Our** house is small. |
| | **your** | Why are you late, girls? Where are **your** bikes? |
| | **their** | They like school. **Their** teacher is nice. |

**Achtung**:

- ***Your*** kann je nach Zusammenhang **dein**, **euer** oder **Ihr** heißen.
- Folgende Formen darfst du nicht verwechseln:

| Possessivbegleiter | Andere Formen |
|---|---|
| **your** | **you're** (Kurzform von *you are*) |
| **his** | **he's** (Kurzform von *he is*/*he has*) |
| **its** | **it's** (Kurzform von *it is*/*it has*) |
| **their** | **they're** (Kurzform von *they are*) |
| **their** | **there** (dort) |

Du entgehst der Verwechslungsgefahr, wenn du daran denkst, dass die Possessivbegleiter (also ***your***, ***his***, ***its*** und ***their***) immer vor einem Substantiv stehen. Sieh dir dazu die folgenden Beispiele an (hervorgehoben sind jeweils die Possessivbegleiter):

You're very funny. I love **your** jokes.
He's too tall for **his** chair. He's got very long legs.
It's a new car. **Its** colour is white.
They're at school, but **their** bags are here.
**Their** things are in the corner over there.

## Aufgabe 6: A lot of noise

**Schreibe auf, was man im Haus von Familie Singasong alles hören kann, und ersetze dabei die unterstrichenen Ausdrücke durch Possessivbegleiter.**

At the Singasongs' house you can hear …

a) Tim's drums ______________________

b) Suzy's keyboards ______________________

c) Dad's guitar ______________________

d) Mum's voice ______________________

e) a bird's song ______________________

f) Tim's and Suzy's shouts (*Rufe*) ______________________

g) the sounds of the washing machine ______________________

h) Lily the cat's purring (*Schnurren*) ______________________

## Aufgabe 7: Many old things

**Tim und Suzy wollen morgen auf dem Flohmarkt einiges verkaufen. Sie besprechen noch einmal, wem welcher Gegenstand gehört. Setze passende Possessivbegleiter in die Lücken ein.**

Suzy: "Mum has got so many shoes. These are (a) ________ shoes, too. But what about this sweatshirt, Tim? Is it (b) ________ sweatshirt?"

Tim: "Yes, it is (c) ________ sweatshirt and I like (d) ________ colour very much. Put it back into (e) ________ room, please."

Suzy: "Okay, now look at Dad's books. (f) ________ books about English grammar are very old. (g) ________ titles (*Buchtitel*) are very boring."

Tim: "You are right, let's sell them. But wait, isn't this (h) ________ parents' new mobile phone, Suzy?"

## Aufgabe 8: Excuses

**Tim und sein Freund Phil sind heute zu spät in den Unterricht gekommen. Und nicht nur deshalb müssen sie sich eine gute Entschuldigung einfallen lassen ...**
**Entscheide, ob du *your*, *you're*, *its* oder *it's* in die Lücken einsetzen musst. Unten steht, wie oft du jeden der Ausdrücke brauchst.**

**you're** (2 ×) – **your** (4 ×) – **it's** (5 ×) – **its** (3 ×)

a) Teacher: "__________ very late, Tim. Is __________ alarm clock out of order (*kaputt*)?"

b) Tim: "Well, __________ not working because __________ batteries are empty. I'm sorry."

c) Teacher: "And what is __________ excuse, Phil? What is __________ reason for being late?"

d) Phil: "__________ my bike, Sir. __________ tyre (*Reifen*) is flat."

e) Teacher: "I see. __________ good at finding excuses. And what about __________ homework, boys?"

f) Phil: "Well, there is a little problem, too. __________ my pen. __________ ink (*Tinte*) has run out."

g) Tim: "I've got my homework, but __________ in my exercise book and the exercise book is not in my school bag. Maybe __________ in my sister's bag. She always takes my things."

## Aufgabe 9: Suzy's cousin

**Suzy stellt ihren Freunden ihren Cousin Oliver vor, der gerade zu Besuch ist. Setze *his* oder *he's* in die Lücken ein.**

This is my cousin. (a) ________ name is Oliver and (b) ________ fourteen. (c) ________ from Wales. (d) ________ here for the weekend. (e) ________ very nice, but (f) ________ accent (*Akzent*) is funny. Look at (g) ________ T-shirt. It shows the Welsh dragon (*Drachen*). (h) ________ older brother is also very nice, but (i) ________ at home in Wales because (j) ________ got a test at university on Monday.

## Aufgabe 10: The London Eye

**Die Singasongs unternehmen mit Oliver einen Ausflug zum London Eye, dem berühmten Riesenrad. Setze *they're*, *their* oder *there* in die Lücken ein.**

(a) ____________ are many people at the London Eye today. Look at Tim and Suzy, (b) ____________ (c) ____________ with (d) ____________ parents, too. (e) ____________ cousin Oliver also wants to go on a ride on the London Eye. (f) ____________ all very excited because it's (g) ____________ first visit to this tourist attraction. When they go up to the top of the big wheel (*Riesenrad*), (h) ____________ very happy. From (i) ____________ they can see the Houses of Parliament. They enjoy (j) ____________ trip to the London Eye very much.

## 2.3 Die Possessivpronomen

### Verwendung und Formen der Possessivpronomen

Die Possessivpronomen (*possessive pronouns*) drücken Besitz oder Zugehörigkeit aus. Sie treten im Satz an die Stelle eines Nomens (Substantivs).

| | | |
|---|---|---|
| Singular | **mine** | This is my bag. It is **mine**. |
| | **yours** | This is your bike. It is **yours**. |
| | **his** | This is his pencil. It is **his**. |
| | **hers** | These are her pictures. They are **hers**. |
| Plural | **ours** | This is our house. It is **ours**. |
| | **yours** | This is your car. It is **yours**. |
| | **theirs** | These are their keys. They are **theirs**. |

Du verwendest Possessivpronomen, wenn das Substantiv bereits bekannt ist und du es nicht wiederholen möchtest.

**Achtung**: Die Form ***its*** wird üblicherweise nicht verwendet.

### Possessivbegleiter und Possessivpronomen im Vergleich

Die Verwendung von Possessivbegleitern und Possessivpronomen entspricht der im Deutschen: Der Begleiter steht **beim** Nomen, das Pronomen steht **anstelle** des Nomens.

| Possessivbegleiter | Possessivpronomen |
|---|---|
| Is this **my** sandwich?<br>Ist das **mein** Sandwich? | Yes, it is **yours**.<br>Ja, es ist **deins**. |

## Aufgabe 11: Your things, my things, our things

**Setze die passenden Possessivpronomen ein.**

a) This is our garden. It is _______________.

b) That's Tim's hat. It is _______________.

c) This is your bag. It is _______________.

d) That is Suzy's coat. It is _______________.

e) This is my diary. It is _______________.

f) That is our neighbours' dog. It is _______________.

## Aufgabe 12: Under the Christmas tree

**Bei Familie Singasong herrscht Chaos unter dem Weihnachtsbaum. So viele Geschenke, doch wem gehört was? Ergänze passende Possessivpronomen.**

Tim: "Thank you so much for this computer game, Dad."

Suzy: "But it isn't (a) ____________, Tim, it is (b) ____________."

Mr Singasong: "That's right, it is for Suzy, so it is (c) ____________."

Mrs Singasong: "And this coffee mug? Is it for Dad?"

Suzy: "Yes, it is (d) ____________."

Mr Singasong: "I like it very much, Suzy, thanks. And this calendar, is it for me and Mum? Is it (e) ____________?"

Suzy: "I don't think it is (f) ____________. Isn't this calendar for Grandma, Tim?"

Tim: "No, it is for Mum and Dad, it is (g) ____________."

## Aufgabe 13: Whose car is it?

**Ein Auto wurde falsch geparkt. Wem gehört es? Streiche jeweils die falsche Angabe durch.**

a) Policeman: "Sorry, is this *your/yours* car, Madam? If it is *your/yours*, please move it away. You must not park here."

b) Mrs Singasong: "No, this isn't *my/mine* car, *my/mine* is much smaller."

c) Policeman: "Is it *your/yours* neighbours' car then? If it is *their/theirs*, you must tell us *their/theirs* names and addresses."

d) Mrs Singasong: "No, it is not *our/ours* neighbours' car."

e) Policeman: "So maybe *your/yours* daughter or *your/yours* son own this car?"

f) Mrs Singasong: "No, it is not *their/theirs*, they are both too young to drive."

g) Policeman: "Okay, but do you know the owner of this car?"

h) Mrs Singasong: "Yes, my mother is here for a cup of tea. The car is *her/hers*."

i) Policeman: "Why didn't you say that earlier?"

## Aufgabe 14: Harry and Jake's problem

**Suzys Mitschüler Harry und Jake haben während des Unterrichts Streit bekommen. Nun sprechen sie mit ihrer Lehrerin Mrs Fair darüber. Setze die unten stehenden Personalpronomen, Possessivbegleiter und Possessivpronomen in die Lücken ein.**

**I – you – he – it – it – it – it – we – us – my – my – your – mine – yours – his – his**

Jake: "Can (a) ________ help (b) ________, please, Mrs Fair?"

Mrs Fair: "What has happened, Jake?"

Jake: "Harry has taken this pen from (c) ________ pencil-case. I'm angry, because the pen is (d) ________ and I want to get (e) ________ back."

Mrs Fair: "So this is Jake's pen, Harry? Is (f) ________ (g) ________ or is (h) ________ (i) ________?"

Harry: "Well, (j) ________ is Harry's pen, that's right. But (k) ________ has written silly things into (l) ________ exercise book with (m) ________ pen and (n) ________ don't like that."

Mrs Fair: "So how can (o) ________ sort out (p) ________ problem, guys? Let's see …"

## 2.4 Demonstrativpronomen und -begleiter

### Die Demonstrativpronomen

- Die Demonstrativpronomen (*demonstrative pronouns*) ***this*** und ***these*** verwendest du, um auf Personen oder Gegenstände zu verweisen, die sich in deiner Nähe befinden. Häufig kannst du dir in solchen Sätzen das Signalwort ***here*** dazudenken.
- Die Demonstrativpronomen ***that*** und ***those*** verwendest du, um auf Personen oder Gegenstände hinzuweisen, die weiter weg sind. Du kannst dir dann häufig das Signalwort ***over there*** dazudenken.

  Look, **this** is my sister **here** and **that** is my brother **over there**.
  **These** are my friends **here** and **those** are my parents **over there**.

### Die Demonstrativbegleiter

***This*/*that*** kannst du auch als Demonstrativbegleiter verwenden. Sie stehen dann vor dem Substantiv. Für die Verwendung gelten die gleichen Regeln wie für ***this*/*that*** als Demonstrativpronomen.

Look at **this** shirt **here**, it is very cheap. Oh, **that** shirt **over there** is also very nice.
I like **these** shoes **here**. And what do you think about **those** trousers **over there**?

## Aufgabe 15: Lost things

**Tim hat gestern einige Dinge im Bus liegen lassen. Deshalb geht er heute ins Fundbüro. Setze *this*, *that*, *these* oder *those* in die Lücken ein.**

a) Tim: "I would like to have a look at ____________ scarf over there. Does it have blue and green stripes?"

b) Clerk (*Angestellter*): "No, it hasn't. But maybe ____________ scarf here is the right one?"

c) Tim: "Oh yes, thanks. I am also looking for my running shoes. No, ____________ here aren't mine."

d) Clerk: "What about ____________ white shoes over there?"

e) Tim: "No, I think my shoes aren't here. But ____________ cap here is mine. Look, there is my name on it."

## Aufgabe 16: Buying clothes

**Die folgenden Sätze benötigst du häufig beim Kleiderkauf. Setze *this*, *that*, *these* oder *those* in die Lücken ein.**

a) Could you please show me ____________ sandals over there?

b) Look at ____________ T-shirt here! Isn't it nice?

c) I would like to see ____________ coat over there, please.

d) Could you please take ____________ jeans here down from the shelf for me?

e) Oh, I really like ____________ jumper here. It's blue, my favourite colour.

f) How much are ____________ boots there in the window?

## 2.5 Die Indefinitpronomen *some, any, no*

Die Wörter ***some*** und ***any*** beziehen sich auf Nomen und bezeichnen eine unbestimmte Menge (*etwas, einige, ein paar*). Man setzt sie unterschiedlich ein:

- ***any*** in Fragen und verneinten Aussagen,
- ***some*** in bejahten/positiven Aussagen.
- In verneinten Aussagen kannst du statt ***not any*** auch ***no*** verwenden.

| | |
|---|---|
| **Fragen** | Have you got **any** milk/postcards?<br>*Haben Sie Milch/Postkarten?* |
| **Bejahte Aussagen** | We can buy **some** milk/postcards.<br>*Wir können (etwas) Milch/(ein paar) Postkarten kaufen.* |
| **Verneinte Aussagen** | They have**n't** got **any** milk/postcards.<br>They have **no** milk/postcards.<br>*Sie haben keine Milch/Postkarten.* |

Wurde das Nomen (z. B. T-shirts) in der Frage bereits genannt, kannst du es im Antwortsatz nach ***some*/*any*** weglassen:

| | |
|---|---|
| Have you got **any** T-shirts? | Yes, I can show you **some**.<br>No, we have**n't** got **any**. |

***Some*** kannst du ausnahmsweise auch in Fragen verwenden, wenn du eine positive Antwort erwartest. Es handelt sich hier eigentlich um Bitten, Angebote oder Vorschläge, die du aus Höflichkeit als Frage verpackst.

Would you like **some** butter, Pam?
Yes, please. And can I have **some** bread, too?

## Aufgabe 17: Let's have dinner

**Tim und Suzy wollen zu Abend essen. Unten siehst du den Inhalt des Kühlschrankes der Familie. Überprüfe, welche der unten angegebenen Lebensmittel darin zu finden sind und welche nicht. Schreibe Sätze mit *some*/*not any* auf.**

Beispiel: a) milk – *There is some milk in the fridge.*

b) orange juice – *But there isn't any orange juice.*

c) cheese
d) bananas
e) spaghetti
f) eggs
g) butter
h) tomatoes
i) ham
j) potatoes
k) yoghurt
l) apples

## Aufgabe 18: A present for a German girl

**Suzy hat regelmäßig Mailkontakt mit Lena, einem Mädchen aus Stuttgart. Sie sucht nun im Kaufhaus nach einem typisch englischen Geschenk, das sie Lena zum Geburtstag schicken will. Setze in Suzys Dialog mit Tim *some* und *any* ein.**

a) Tim: "Why don't you buy ___________ tea for Lena?"

b) Suzy: "Tea is fine but there isn't ___________ in this shop here."

c) Tim: "What about ___________ crackers then?"

d) Suzy: "I don't know if Lena likes crackers. Don't you have ___________ other ideas?"

e) Tim: "Well, does this shop have ___________ cups with pictures of the Royal family (*königliche Familie*)?"

f) Suzy: "No, I can't see ___________."

g) Tim: "Let's look for ___________ funny cards then."

h) Suzy: "Okay, and maybe I'll find ___________ nice pencils with the British flag on them."

## Aufgabe 19: How to be polite

**Formuliere mithilfe der folgenden Bausteine mindestens sechs höfliche Fragen und Bitten, wie man sie z. B. beim Essen mit der Familie verwendet.**

| | | | |
|---|---|---|---|
| Would you like<br>Can I give you<br>Can I please have<br>Could you please pass me | some | water<br>salt<br>bread<br>lemonade<br>potatoes<br>beans (*Bohnen*)<br>sauce<br>ketchup | ? |

# Abschlusstest online 2

Glückwunsch! Du hast das **Kapitel 2 – Pronomen und Begleiter** durchgearbeitet. Jetzt ist dir klarer, wann es **he** und wann **him** heißen muss und wie du mit **his** anzeigst, was jemandem gehört. Mit den Demonstrativpronomen und -begleitern kannst du außerdem sprachlich auf Menschen und Dinge hindeuten.

**So funktioniert der Abschlusstest online:**
Um deinen Lernerfolg zu überprüfen, kannst du nun die Abschlusstests machen. Gehe auf
**https://www.klett-lerntraining.de/9Y2A**
und wähle das Kapitel und einen Test aus.

Welche Tests es gibt, siehst du unten in der Tabelle. Nach jedem Test bekommst du eine Auswertung.

Willst du immer im Blick haben, welche Themen du schon kannst oder was du besser wiederholen solltest? Dann schreibe deine Ergebnisse in die Tabelle.

## Mein Ergebnis im Abschlusstest online – Kapitel 2

| Thema | Mein Ergebnis |
|---|---|
| Subjektform und Objektform der Personalpronomen | |
| Die Possessivbegleiter und Possessivpronomen | |
| Demonstrativpronomen und -begleiter | |
| Die Indefinitpronomen *some*, *any*, *no* | |

# 3 Das *present tense*

## 3.1 Bejahte Formen im *simple present*

### *To be* und *to have got*

Das *simple present* ist die einfache Gegenwartsform im Englischen. Die Formen für die beiden wichtigen Verben *to be* und *to have got* lauten so:

| | **to be** | | **to have got** | |
|---|---|---|---|---|
| | Langform | Kurzform | Langform | Kurzform |
| Singular | I **am** | I'**m** | I **have got** | I'**ve got** |
| | you **are** | you'**re** | you **have got** | you'**ve got** |
| | he **is** | he'**s** | he **has got** | he'**s got** |
| | she **is** | she'**s** | she **has got** | she'**s got** |
| | it **is** | it'**s** | it **has got** | it'**s got** |
| Plural | we **are** | we'**re** | we **have got** | we'**ve got** |
| | you **are** | you'**re** | you **have got** | you'**ve got** |
| | they **are** | they'**re** | they **have got** | they'**ve got** |

- Die Langform verwendest du, wenn du etwas schreibst.
- Die Kurzform verwendest du, wenn du sprichst, Gespräche aufschreibst oder an Freunde schreibst.

**Achtung, diese beiden Formen sind leicht zu verwechseln:**

He'**s** got a new mobile.
(Kurzform von *has got*)

He'**s** new in our tutor group.
(Kurzform von *is*)

### Andere Vollverben

Das *simple present*, die einfache Gegenwart, hat bei den anderen Vollverben die gleiche Form wie der Infinitiv des Verbs. In der 3. Person Singular (bei *he*, *she* und *it*) muss an diese Form ein **s** angehängt werden.

| | | |
|---|---|---|
| Singular | I | read |
| | you | read |
| | he/she/it | read**s** |
| Plural | we | read |
| | you | read |
| | they | read |

**Besonderheiten bei der Schreibung der 3. Person Singular:**

- Nach Zischlauten wie [ʃ, tʃ] wird **es** angehängt:
  He always watch**es** the news.
- Auch an *go* und *do* wird **es** angehängt:
  He go**es** to work. He do**es** his job.
- Bei Konsonant + y am Wortende wird **y** zu **ies** (aber nicht bei Vokal + y):
  They fly to Germany, but he fl**ies** to New York.
  Aber: I say something and he sa**ys** something else.

## Aufgabe 1: Tim's life

**Setze die passenden Formen von *to be* und *to have* im *simple present* ein.**

a) I ____________ Tim. I ____________ got a sister.

b) Suzy ____________ funny. She ____________ got a lot of humour (*Humor*).

c) Sometimes we ____________ got problems and we ____________ angry at each other.

d) Sometimes I ____________ got trouble with my parents, but luckily (*glücklicherweise*) they ____________ got strong nerves.

e) School ____________ okay. All of my friends ____________ there, too.

f) One girl ____________ really nice, she ____________ got blue eyes.

## Aufgabe 2: A quiz about animals

**Setze die unten stehenden Verben im *simple present* in die Lücken ein. Nenne anschließend das Tier, um das es geht.**

**work – carry – laugh – be – be – call – sound – live**

a) I ________________ a very big animal.

b) My voice ________________ like a trumpet.

c) I ________________ in Africa or in Asia.

d) The colour of my skin ________________ grey.

e) You ________________ my nose a "trunk".

f) I ________________ heavy things or people on my back.

g) Some of my brothers and sisters ________________ in circuses.

h) Silly people ________________ about my ears.

The name of the animal: ________________

## Aufgabe 3: Another animal quiz

**Schreibe die Sätze im *simple present* in der richtigen Reihenfolge in dein Heft. Nenne anschließend das Tier, um das es geht.**

a) live – in the house or in the garden – I

b) be – long walks – good for me

c) your best friend – be – I

d) I – the postman (*Briefträger*) – bark at

e) cats – nasty – find – I

The name of the animal: ________________

## Aufgabe 4: Mr Singasong's spaghetti sauce

**In der Wörterschlange stehen die Verben, die du für die Lücken benötigst. Markiere zunächst die Wortgrenzen. Die Verben stehen bereits in der richtigen Reihenfolge, aber im Infinitiv. Setze sie im *simple present* in die Lücken ein.**

behavegotturnsinggoneedcutheatputaddcookfeel

a) Mr Singasong ________________ a very good cook.

b) He ________________ his own recipe (*Rezept*) for a spaghetti sauce.

c) First he ________________ on the music.

d) He ________________ an Italian song.

e) Then he ________________ into the garden …

f) … because he ________________ some basil (*Basilikum*).

g) Next he ________________ an onion and some garlic into small pieces.

h) Then he ________________ some oil in a frying pan (*Pfanne*).

i) He ________________ the onion and the garlic into the hot oil.

j) After that he ________________ a tin of tomatoes, salt, pepper and the basil.

k) Finally he ________________ the spaghetti in a big pot.

l) Now he ________________ ready for another Italian song.

## 3.2 Verneinung im *simple present*

### Verneinung von *to be* und *to have got*

Auch für die Verneinung von *to be* und *to have got* stehen dir Lang- und Kurzformen zur Verfügung.

**Langformen:**

| | **to be** | **to have got** |
|---|---|---|
| Singular | I **am not** | I **have not got** |
| | you **are not** | you **have not got** |
| | he/she/it **is not** | he/she/it **has not got** |
| Plural | we **are not** | we **have not got** |
| | you **are not** | you **have not got** |
| | they **are not** | they **have not got** |

Die Verneinung der Langformen bildest du

- bei ***to be***: indem du ***not*** nach ***am/is/are*** einsetzt.
- bei ***to have got***: indem du ***not*** zwischen ***have/has*** und ***got*** einsetzt.

**Kurzformen der Verneinung:**

| | **to be** | **to have got** |
|---|---|---|
| Singular | I**'m not** | I **haven't got** |
| | you **aren't** | you **haven't got** |
| | he/she/it **isn't** | he/she/it **hasn't got** |
| Plural | we **aren't** | we **haven't got** |
| | you **aren't** | you **haven't got** |
| | they **aren't** | they **haven't got** |

Bei den verneinten Kurzformen wird

- ***not*** mit ***are/is*** zusammengezogen zu ***aren't/isn't***,
- ***not*** mit ***have/has*** zusammengezogen zu ***haven't/hasn't***.

**Achtung, Ausnahme**: die verneinte Kurzform I**'m not**

### Verneinung von anderen Vollverben

Gibt es in einem Satz keine Hilfsverben und keine Form von *to be*, sondern nur ein Vollverb, dann bildet man die Verneinung mit ***to do.*** Die Form von *to do* wird vor das Vollverb gestellt. Das Vollverb selbst steht im Infinitiv. Du hängst also in der 3. Person Singular **kein s** an!

| | | | |
|---|---|---|---|
| Singular | I | **do not** | |
| | you | **do not** | |
| | he/she/it | **does not** | read |
| Plural | we | **do not** | |
| | you | **do not** | |
| | they | **do not** | |

Die Kurzformen lauten don't/doesn't:

I **don't** read. He **doesn't** read.

## Aufgabe 5: You aren't silly

**Bilde Sätze mit der verneinten Form von *to be*.**

Beispiel: a) you – not silly – *You aren't silly.*

b) she – not tall ____________________

c) I – not small ____________________

d) he – not young ____________________

e) it – not new ____________________

f) they – not nice ____________________

g) we – not old ____________________

## Aufgabe 6: They haven't got a house

**Bilde Sätze mit der verneinten Form von *to have got*.**

Beispiel: a) they – not – a house – *They haven't got a house.*

b) I – not – a pencil ______________________________

c) she – not – a ball ______________________________

d) we – not – a car ______________________________

e) he – not – a game ______________________________

f) you – not – a sandwich ______________________________

g) it – not – a door ______________________________

## Aufgabe 7: A lazy Sunday

**Suche dir aus den unten stehenden Verben die passenden heraus und bilde die Verneinung mit *to do*, um herauszufinden, was bei Familie Singasong an Sonntagen alles anders ist als sonst.**

**not get up – not tell – not spend – not drive – not bring – not eat – not go**

a) Mr Singasong ______________________________ at 6 o'clock.

b) Mrs Singasong ______________________________ her taxi.

c) Tim and Suzy ______________________________ to school.

d) Mrs Singasong ______________________ her children to hurry up.

e) The cat Lily ______________________ so much time on her own.

f) The postman ______________________ the family any letters.

g) Tim and Suzy ______________________ at the school cafeteria.

## Aufgabe 8: A bad time

**Wie verhält sich Tim, wenn er Krach mit seinen Eltern hat? Bilde verneinte Sätze im *simple present*.**

Beispiel: a) not talk to his parents – *Tim doesn't talk to his parents.*

b) not open the door of his room ______________________

c) not have dinner with his family ______________________

d) not turn off the music in his room ______________________

e) not answer the phone ______________________

f) not come into the living room ______________________

g) not do his homework ______________________

## Aufgabe 9: Not their cup of tea (nicht ihr Ding)

**Es gibt einiges, wofür sich Suzys Mitschüler nicht interessieren. Bilde die Verneinung der angegebenen Verben im *simple present*.**

a) Olivia ______________________ (not be) interested in playing basketball.

b) Daniel ______________________ (not play) computer games.

c) Olivia and Daniel ______________________ (not collect) magazines.

d) Ruby ______________________ (not have got) a guitar.

e) George ______________________ (not go) swimming.

f) Ruby and George ______________________ (not have got) a skateboard.

g) Lucas ______________________ (not draw) pictures.

h) Sophie ______________________ (not like) running.

i) Lucas and Sophie ______________________ (not watch) videos.

j) Most of them ______________________ (not be) interested in knitting (*Stricken*).

## 3.3 Bejahte und verneinte Formen des *present progressive*

Für jede Zeitstufe gibt es im Englischen zwei verschiedene Formen, die man unterschiedlich gebraucht: eine einfache Form (*simple form*) und eine Verlaufsform (*progressive form*).

### Bejahte Formen

***Present progressive*** ist die Bezeichnung für die Verlaufsform der Gegenwart. Sie drückt aus, dass etwas gerade geschieht.

Sie wird gebildet aus einer Form von ***to be*** und der ***ing*-Form,** also dem Infinitiv des Vollverbs + *ing*.

| | | | |
|---|---|---|---|
| Singular | I | **am** | |
| | you | **are** | |
| | he/she/it | **is** | **reading** |
| Plural | we | **are** | |
| | you | **are** | |
| | they | **are** | |

### Verneinte Formen

Bei der Verneinung wird entweder ***not*** nach der Form von *to be* eingefügt oder die entsprechende Kurzform verwendet:

He is **not** watching TV.
She is**n't** playing a computer game.

### Besonderheiten bei der Schreibung der *ing*-Form

- Ein stummes e am Ende des Verbs fällt weg.

  tak**e** + *ing* → tak**ing**
  writ**e** + *ing* → writ**ing**

- Endet das Verb auf Konsonant nach einem betonten Kurzvokal, verdoppelt sich der Konsonant.

  ru**n** + *ing* → ru**nning**
  ge**t** + *ing* → ge**tting**

## Aufgabe 10: How to get there

**Sortiere die Buchstaben dieser Fortbewegungsverben und bilde die *ing*-Form.**

a) ______________________ (klaw)

b) ______________________ (nru)

c) ______________________ (deir) a bike

d) ______________________ (iswm)

e) ______________________ (lfy)

f) ______________________ (ivdr) a car

g) ______________________ (aket) a bus

## Aufgabe 11: An evening with the scouts

**Was Tim und Suzy gerade bei den Pfadfindern erleben, erfährst du, wenn du die unten stehenden Verben im *present progressive* einsetzt.**

**play – eat – have – talk – sit – laugh – roast – look**

a) They ______________________ around a fire.

b) Tim ______________________ the guitar.

c) They ______________________ marshmallows in the fire.

d) Suzy ______________________ about a joke.

e) Tim's friend Nat ______________________ some bread.

f) Nat and Suzy ______________________ about their plans.

g) Suzy ______________________ into the flames.

h) All of them ______________________ a good time.

## Aufgabe 12: On the beach

**Setze die Verben in Klammern ins *present progressive*.**

a) The Singasongs ______________________________ (spend) a weekend at the seaside in Brighton.

b) They ______________________________ (have) a lot of fun on the beach.

c) Tim ______________________________ (chase) Suzy in the water.

d) Mrs Singasong ______________________________ (buy) some ice-cream.

e) Mr Singasong ______________________________ (read) a book.

f) A lot of other people ______________________________ (enjoy: *genießen*) their time on the beach, too.

g) A little child ______________________________ (build) a sand castle.

h) An old man ______________________________ (try) to catch a fish.

i) A girl ______________________________ (drink) a bottle of water.

j) Another girl ______________________________ (draw) a picture of the sea.

k) A woman ______________________________ (sleep) on her sunbed (*Liegestuhl*).

l) A boy ______________________________ (look) at a sailing boat.

m) His brother ______________________________ (call) his girl-friend.

n) Some teenagers ______________________________ (play) volleyball.

o) A dog ______________________________ (swim) in the water.

## Aufgabe 13: Things they are doing

**Schreibe auf, was die Personen/Tiere gerade tun beziehungsweise nicht tun.**

Beispiel: a) *Tim is smiling. He isn't crying.*

a) Tim smile/cry

b) Suzy swim/sail

c) A dog sleep/bark

d) Tim and Suzy run/jump

e) Lily and a dog play/fight

f) Lily climb a tree/fall down

g) Tim eat/cook

h) Suzy watch TV/do sports

i) Tim and Suzy leave the house/arrive

## 3.4 Der Gebrauch von *simple present* und *present progressive*

### Verwendung des *simple present*

In diesen Fällen verwendest du das *simple present*:

- Etwas ist eine allgemeingültige Tatsache:

  The earth **moves** around the sun.

- Etwas geschieht häufig, regelmäßig oder aus Gewohnheit:

  I **go** to school every day.

  **Signalwörter**: *always, sometimes, often, usually, never, every day, every month, every year; on Mondays, on Tuesdays etc.*

- Mehrere Dinge geschehen nacheinander (z. B. in einer Erzählung, Inhaltsangabe oder einer Anleitung):

  First Kylie **gets** up. Then she **has** breakfast. After that she **goes** to school.

  **Signalwörter**: *first, then, after that, finally*

### Verwendung des *present progressive*

In diesen Fällen verwendest du das *present progressive*:

- Etwas geschieht gerade und ist noch nicht abgeschlossen:

  Look, Tim **is writing** a mail now.

  **Signalwörter**: *now, just, this morning, this evening, today, look!*

**Das musst du außerdem beachten:**

- Im Deutschen gibt es keine Verlaufsform. Wir übersetzen die englische Form daher häufig mit „gerade" oder „im Moment":

  John **is watching** TV. John schaut **gerade** fern.

- Hilfsverben wie *can, must, have got* bilden keine Verlaufsform. Auch die Verben *to be, to like, to hate* und *to want* werden fast immer im *simple present* verwendet.

## Aufgabe 14: Lily at home alone

**Lily, die Katze der Familie Singasong, ist allein zu Haus. Entscheide, ob du das *simple present* oder das *present progressive* der angegebenen Verben in die Lücken einsetzen musst.**

a) Lily ______________________ (like) milk a lot.

b) Look, she ______________________ (drink) her milk now.

c) She ______________________ (be) very thirsty.

d) So she ______________________ (want) some more.

e) But she ______________________ (not can) get more milk,

f) because there ______________________ (be) nobody at home.

g) Now Lily ______________________ (try) to open the fridge,

h) but she ______________________ (not can) do that.

i) So she ______________________ (must) think of something else.

j) First she ______________________ (have) a look at the breakfast table.

k) But there ______________________ (not be) any milk left (übrig).

l) Then she ______________________ (climb: *klettern*) onto the cupboard in the living room.

m) But she ______________________ (not be) lucky.

n) Finally she ______________________ (not know) what else (*was noch*) to try.

o) Now she ______________________ (wait) until the Singasongs come home.

## Aufgabe 15: An unusual (ungewöhnlich) holiday

**Hier erfährst du, wie Familie Singasong ihren Urlaub normalerweise verbringt. Aber dieses Mal ist einiges anders. Entscheide jeweils, ob du das *simple present* oder das *present progressive* brauchst.**

a) Usually the Singasongs ______________________ (spend) their holidays at the sea, but this time they ______________________ (stay) in the Lake District (*englisches Urlaubsgebiet mit Seen und Bergen*).

b) Every August they ______________________ (relax: *sich entspannen*) on the beach, but this August they ______________________ (take) long walks in the mountains.

c) They often ______________________ (rise: *aufstehen*) late in their holidays, but today they ______________________ (get up) at seven.

d) This year they ______________________ (stay) at a friend's house, but usually they ______________________ (go) to a hotel.

e) Normally they ______________________ (eat) their dinner at a restaurant in their holidays, but this time Mr Singasong ______________________ (do) the cooking.

f) This year they ______________________ (buy) a lot of souvenirs, but usually they ______________________ (not do) a lot of shopping in their holidays.

g) Normally they ______________________ (not take) the bus in their holidays, but today they ______________________ (go) to Windermere, a small village, by bus.

# Abschlusstest online 3

Super! Du hast das **Kapitel 3 – Das *present tense*** durchgearbeitet. Dabei hast du die beiden Möglichkeiten wiederholt, wie du auf Englisch über das sprechen kannst, was in der Gegenwart passiert: mit dem *simple present* über Dinge, die regelmäßig ablaufen oder allgemeingültig sind, mit dem *present progressive* über Sachen, die jetzt in diesem Moment geschehen.

**So funktioniert der Abschlusstest online:**
Um deinen Lernerfolg zu überprüfen, kannst du nun die Abschlusstests machen. Gehe auf
**https://www.klett-lerntraining.de/9Y2A**
und wähle das Kapitel und einen Test aus.

Welche Tests es gibt, siehst du unten in der Tabelle. Nach jedem Test bekommst du eine Auswertung.

Willst du immer im Blick haben, welche Themen du schon kannst oder was du besser wiederholen solltest? Dann schreibe deine Ergebnisse in die Tabelle.

## Mein Ergebnis im Abschlusstest online – Kapitel 3

| Thema | Mein Ergebnis |
|---|---|
| Bejahte und verneinte Formen im *simple present* | |
| Bejahte und verneinte Formen im *present progressive* | |
| Der Gebrauch von *simple present* und *present progressive* | |

# 4 Das *past tense*

## 4.1 Bejahte Formen im *simple past*

### Regelmäßige Verben

Die einfache Form der Vergangenheit, das ***simple past***, verwendest du, wenn du über abgeschlossene Vorgänge in der Vergangenheit sprichst.

Bei den regelmäßigen Verben (*regular verbs*) hängst du die Endung **ed** an den Infinitiv an:

play + ed → played

Die Formen des *simple past* lauten für alle Personen gleich:

| | | |
|---|---|---|
| Singular | I | |
| | you | |
| | he/she/it | **played** |
| Plural | we | |
| | you | |
| | they | |

**Regeln zur Schreibung:**

- Ein **stummes e** am Ende des Verbs fällt weg:

  lik**e** + ed → liked

- Nach **Konsonant +** y am Wortende wird y zu **i**:

  tr**y** + ed → tr**i**ed

- Ein **Konsonant am Wortende**, der nach einem betonten Kurzvokal steht, verdoppelt sich:

  sto**p** + ed → sto**pp**ed

### Unregelmäßige Verben

Einige Verben bilden die Vergangenheit unregelmäßig (*irregular verbs*), z. B.:

| | | | |
|---|---|---|---|
| make | → | **made** | He **made** a mistake yesterday. |
| take | → | **took** | She **took** a lot of money with her. |
| go | → | **went** | They **went** to the park. |

Diese Formen musst du lernen. Ein Verzeichnis findest du sicher in deinem Englischbuch.

Auch bei den unregelmäßigen Verben lauten die Formen für alle Personen gleich. Die einzige Ausnahme ist das Verb ***to be***:

| | | |
|---|---|---|
| Singular | I | **was** |
| | you | **were** |
| | he/she/it | **was** |
| Plural | we | **were** |
| | you | **were** |
| | they | **were** |

## Aufgabe 1: Things the teacher did yesterday

**Setze die Verben in Klammern im *simple past* in die Lücken ein.**

a) The English teacher ______________________ (explain) a grammar rule.

b) She ______________________ (correct) a wrong answer.

c) She ______________________ (copy) a work sheet (*Arbeitsblatt*).

d) She ______________________ (count) the points in a test.

e) She ______________________ (play) a game with the pupils.

f) She ______________________ (repeat) some of the exercises.

g) She ______________________ (practise) the spelling of a few words with the pupils.

## Aufgabe 2: A criss-cross puzzle with irregular verbs

**Setze die angegebenen Verben im *simple past* in das Kreuzworträtsel ein.**

Across (*waagrecht*):

3 fight

4 buy

5 say

6 take

9 give

10 meet

Down (*senkrecht*):

1 bring

2 write

3 find

5 speak

7 keep

8 come

## Aufgabe 3: At the fun park

**In der Wörterschlange stehen die Verben, die du für die Lücken benötigst. Markiere zunächst die Wortgrenzen. Die Verben stehen bereits in der richtigen Reihenfolge. Setze sie im *simple past* in die Lücken ein.**

goberidewantbelikewatcheatfeelenjoydrivecostdohave

a) Last week Tim and Suzy ______________________ to the fun park.

b) There ______________________ many exciting activities to do.

c) First, they ______________________ down a very fast slide (*Rutsche*).

d) Then they ______________________ to ride the ghost train (*Geisterbahn*).

e) Inside, Suzy ______________________ a little scared.

f) She ______________________ the Western Town much.

g) They ______________________ a show about the Wild West there.

h) Tim ______________________ a lot of popcorn during the show.

i) Later, he ______________________ sick because of it.

j) Both of them ______________________ the ride with the roller-coaster (*Achterbahn*).

k) They also ______________________ small gokarts.

l) All of that ______________________ a lot of money, of course.

m) But that ______________________ not matter to them …

n) … because they ______________________ a brilliant day.

## 4.2 Verneinung des *simple past*

### Die Verneinung von *to be* im *simple past*

Zur Verneinung des *simple past* von *to be* setzt du ***not*** nach der entsprechenden Form von ***to be*** ein:

He **was not** ready. She **was not** tired.

Auch hier gibt es eine Langform und eine Kurzform:

| | | Langform | Kurzform |
|---|---|---|---|
| Singular | I | was not | wasn't |
| | you | were not | weren't |
| | he/she/it | was not | wasn't |
| Plural | we | were not | weren't |
| | you | were not | weren't |
| | they | were not | weren't |

### Die Verneinung von anderen Vollverben im *simple past*

Andere Vollverben verneinst du im *simple past*, indem du ***did not*** einfügst. Denke daran, dass das Vollverb im Infinitiv steht!

| | | | |
|---|---|---|---|
| Singular | I | | |
| | you | | |
| | he/she/it | **did not** | read |
| Plural | we | | |
| | you | | |
| | they | | |

Die Kurzform von ***did not*** lautet ***didn't***.

*Did not/didn't* ist die Vergangenheitsform von *do not/don't* und von *does not/doesn't*. Sie lautet also **für alle Personen gleich**.

## Aufgabe 4: A lot of problems

**Oft beschweren sich Leute nach ihrem Urlaub über Dinge, mit denen sie nicht zufrieden waren. Formuliere solche Beschwerden mithilfe der Verneinung von *to be* im *simple past*.**

Beispiel: a) the waiters – not friendly: The waiters weren't friendly.

b) the hotel room – not clean ______________________

c) the swimming pool – not warm enough ______________________

d) the weather – not good ______________________

e) the prices – not cheap ______________________

f) the hotel – not close to the sea ______________________

g) the shops – not interesting ______________________

## Aufgabe 5: A forgetful teacher

**Setze die Verben in Klammern im *simple past* in die Lücken ein.**

a) Last week the English teacher ______________________ (not feel) very well.

b) So she ______________________ (not remember) everything that was important.

c) She ______________________ (not put) her English book into her bag.

d) She ______________________ (not take) her school keys with her.

e) She ______________________ (not find) her watch.

f) She ______________________ (not control) the pupils' homework.

## Aufgabe 6: Stephen McSpooky

**Eines der Lieblingsbücher von Suzy handelt von Stephen McSpooky, einem fünfhundert Jahre alten Geist in Schottland. Der hatte einige Probleme … Setze die Verben in der verneinten Form des *simple past* in die Lücken ein.**

a) Stephen's castle ______________________________ (not look) scary.

b) There ______________________________ (not be) any cobwebs (*Spinnweben*) there.

c) He ______________________________ (not use) candles but electric light.

d) Tourists ______________________________ (not come) to his castle.

e) He ______________________________ (not know) what to do all day.

f) His skin ______________________________ (not be) pale (*bleich*) enough.

g) He ______________________________ (not scare) anyone.

h) Even the mice ______________________________ (not be) afraid of him.

i) He ______________________________ (not enjoy) walking around in his castle at night.

j) He ______________________________ (not seem) like a real ghost.

## Aufgabe 7: One hundred years ago

**Setze die unten stehenden Verben in der verneinten Form des *simple past* in die Lücken ein.**

**not use – not be – not read – not chat – not take – not travel – not send – not help – not make – not fly – not be – not give**

a) One hundred years ago people ______________________ their phone calls with mobile phones.

b) They ______________________ with their friends on the world wide web.

c) Pupils ______________________ notebook computers to present their ideas at school.

d) They ______________________ stories in digital books (*E-Bücher*).

e) There ______________________ any mp3 players.

f) People ______________________ photos with digital cameras.

g) They ______________________ any text messages to their friends.

h) Robots ______________________ building cars in car factories.

i) There ______________________ any navigation systems in cars.

j) Planes ______________________ around the world within two days.

k) Satellites ______________________ people any information about the weather.

l) People ______________________ to the moon.

## 4.3 Das *past progressive*

Die Verlaufsform der Vergangenheit, das ***past progressive***, drückt aus, dass eine Handlung zu einem bestimmten Zeitpunkt in der Vergangenheit noch andauerte.

Genau wie das *present progressive* bildet man das *past progressive* aus einer Form von *to be*, in diesem Fall ***was*/*were***, und der ***ing*-Form**.

| | | | | |
|---|---|---|---|---|
| Singular | I | **was** | | |
| | you | **were** | | |
| | he/she/it | **was** | **(not)** | **listening** |
| Plural | we | **were** | | |
| | you | **were** | | |
| | they | **were** | | |

Für die Verneinung setzt du ***not*** nach ***was*/*were*** ein. Du kannst auch die entsprechenden Kurzformen ***wasn't*/*weren't*** verwenden:

It **wasn't** raining. They **weren't** playing.

### Aufgabe 8: We were walking

**Bilde kurze Sätze im *past progressive*.**

Beispiel: a) we – walk: *We were walking.*

b) you – run ____________________

c) I – jump ____________________

d) he – go ____________________

e) they – turn ____________________

f) she – stop ____________________

g) it – move ____________________

## Aufgabe 9: A strange world

**Letzte Nacht hat Tim von einer Welt geträumt, in der alles verkehrt herum funktioniert. Setze die Verben in Klammern in die bejahte oder verneinte Form des *past progressive*, und du erfährst, wie es in dieser Welt zuging.**

a) In Tim's dream he ______________________ (not walk) on the floor, he ______________________ (walk) on the ceiling.

b) Cats ______________________ (not eat) mice, but mice ______________________ (eat) cats.

c) People ______________________ (drive) their cars only backwards (*rückwärts*). They ______________________ (not drive) straight ahead (*vorwärts*).

d) Mrs Singasong ______________________ (not wear) a hat on her head, but she ______________________ (wear) a hat on her feet.

e) Tim and Suzy ______________________ (not go) to school, but their parents ______________________ (go) to school.

f) Tim and Suzy's parents ______________________ (not tell) their children what to do, but Tim and Suzy ______________________ (tell) their parents what to do.

g) Fish ______________________ (not swim) in water. They ______________________ (swim) in the garden.

h) Birds ______________________ (not fly) through the air, they ______________________ (fly) through water.

i) People ______________________ (not laughing) when they were happy, they ______________________ (cry).

## 4.4 Der Gebrauch von *simple past* und *past progressive*

### Die Verwendung des *simple past*

- Mit dem *simple past* kannst du über abgeschlossene Handlungen in der Vergangenheit berichten.

  Tom **went** to Mike's birthday party **yesterday**.

  **Signalwörter**: *yesterday, last week, last year, in the morning, in the evening* etc.

  Auch *when* ist ein Signalwort für das *simple past*, es leitet Nebensätze ein:

  **When** I **finished** work, it **was** already 10 pm.

### Die Verwendung des *past progressive*

- Das *past progressive* betont die Dauer einer Handlung in der Vergangenheit.

  We **were swimming** all morning.

- Es wird verwendet für Handlungen, die zu einem bestimmten Zeitpunkt in der Vergangenheit andauerten und noch nicht abgeschlossen waren.

  At 8 pm he **was listening** to music.

- Das *past progressive* betont, dass eine Handlung noch andauerte, während eine neue Handlung einsetzte. Diese neue Handlung steht im *simple past*!

  I **was** still **eating** my lunch when my brother arrived.

  **Signalwörter**: *still, just, while*

## Aufgabe 10: At the museum

**Suzys Klasse unternimmt einen Ausflug in ein großes Museum. Entscheide, ob du die Verben in Klammern ins *simple past* oder *past progressive* setzen musst.**

a) Suzy and her classmates ______________________________ (chat) excitedly when they ______________________________ (leave) school together.

b) The teacher ______________________________ (tell) the pupils to be quiet when they ______________________________ (arrive) at the museum.

c) While the group ______________________________ (walk) around the museum, the light ______________________________ (go) out suddenly.

d) While some pupils ______________________________ (scream), others ______________________________ (be) quiet.

e) Everybody ______________________________ (feel) better when the blackout (*Stromausfall*) ______________________________ ______________________ (be) over.

f) Suzy ______________________________ (take) a picture while she ______________________________ (look) at the Egyptian mummies (*ägyptische Mumien*).

g) She ______________________________ (listen) to an audio guide when her friend ______________________________ (ask) her to go to the cafeteria of the museum.

h) While they ______________________________ (have) a cup of tea in the cafeteria, their teacher ______________________ (look) for them.

## Aufgabe 11: A runaway (Ausreißer)

**Entscheide, ob du die Verben in Klammern ins *simple past* oder ins *past progressive* setzen musst.**

Last year the Singasongs' cat Lily (a) ______________________ (make) a new friend: the dog Leo. Leo (b) ______________________ (run) around the streets on his own when he (c) ______________________ (come) past the house of the Singasong family. While he (d) ______________________ (cross) the street, he (e) ______________________ (watch) another dog. So he (f) __________ __________ (not see) Tim, who (g) __________ __________ (ride) home from a friend on his skateboard. Luckily (*glücklicherweise*), Tim (h) ______________________ (stop) in time (*rechtzeitig*) and (i) ______________________ (not hurt) Leo. But Leo (j) ______________________ (be) so shocked that he (k) ______________________ (not move) anymore.
He (l) ______________________ (not bark) while Tim (m) ______________________ (carry) him into the Singasongs' house. There Tim (n) ______________________ (put) him on the floor, next to Lily's basket.
Leo (o) ______________________ (open) his eyes again when Lily (p) ______________________ (touch) his paw (*Pfote*). Tim (q) __________ __________ (be) very happy about this.
He (r) __________ __________ (look) at the dog for injuries when he (s) ______________________ (find) a phone number on Leo's collar (*Halsband*). Finally a nice old lady (t) ______________________ (fetch) Leo, the runaway.



WISSEN ÜBEN TESTEN

# Abschlusstest online 4

Tolle Leistung! Du hast das **Kapitel 4 – Das *past tense*** durchgearbeitet. Dabei hast du dir wieder ins Gedächtnis gerufen, dass es im Englischen mehrere Vergangenheitsformen gibt: Mit dem *simple past* werden abgeschlossene Handlungen in der Vergangenheit ausgedrückt, mit dem *past progressive* solche, die in der Vergangenheit noch andauerten, als ein anderes Ereignis eintrat.

**So funktioniert der Abschlusstest online:**
Um deinen Lernerfolg zu überprüfen, kannst du nun die Abschlusstests machen. Gehe auf
**https://www.klett-lerntraining.de/9Y2A**
und wähle das Kapitel und einen Test aus.

Welche Tests es gibt, siehst du unten in der Tabelle. Nach jedem Test bekommst du eine Auswertung.

Willst du immer im Blick haben, welche Themen du schon kannst oder was du besser wiederholen solltest? Dann schreibe deine Ergebnisse in die Tabelle.

## Mein Ergebnis im Abschlusstest online – Kapitel 4

| Thema | Mein Ergebnis |
|---|---|
| Bejahte und verneinte Formen im *simple past* | |
| Bejahte und verneinte Formen im *past progressive* | |
| Der Gebrauch von *simple past* und *past progressive* | |

# 5 Das *present perfect*

## 5.1 Bejahte und verneinte Formen des *present perfect*

Das ***present perfect*** drückt aus, dass etwas in der Vergangenheit geschehen ist, die Auswirkung oder das Ergebnis aber noch spürbar ist. Außerdem wird es verwendet, wenn eine Handlung gerade erst abgeschlossen wurde.
Für die Bildung brauchst du das ***past participle.***

### Das *past participle* der regelmäßigen Verben

Bei regelmäßigen Verben wird das *past participle* wie das *simple past* aus dem **Infinitiv des Verbs + ed** gebildet:

play + ed → play**ed**

Bei der Schreibung musst du folgende Besonderheiten beachten:

- Ein stummes **e** am Ende des Verbs fällt weg:

  lik**e** + ed → (have/has) liked

- Bei Verben mit **Konsonant + y** am Wortende wird **y** zu **i**:

  tr**y** + ed → (have/has) tr**ied**

- Ein **Konsonant am Ende des Verbs**, der nach einem betonten Kurzvokal steht, verdoppelt sich:

  sto**p** + ed → (have/has) sto**pp**ed

### Das *past participle* der unregelmäßigen Verben

Die unregelmäßigen Formen des *past participle* musst du lernen. Du findest sicher eine Übersicht in deinem Englischbuch. Beispiele:

make → **made**  take → **taken**

### Die Bildung des *present perfect*

Das ***present perfect*** bildest du aus ***have*/*has*** und dem ***past participle***.

| | | | | |
|---|---|---|---|---|
| Singular | I | **have** | | |
| | you | **have** | | |
| | he/she/it | **has** | **(not)** | **played** |
| Plural | we | **have** | | |
| | you | **have** | | |
| | they | **have** | | |

Die **Verneinung** bildest du, indem du **not** nach **have/has** einsetzt.

Du kannst in bejahten und verneinten Sätzen auch die entsprechenden Kurzformen verwenden:

I'**ve** talked to my friend. He **hasn't** had lunch yet.

## Aufgabe 1: She has arrived

**Schreibe kurze Aussagesätze im *present perfect*.**

Beispiel: a) she – arrive: *She has arrived.*

b) he – leave c) I – start d) you – stop e) we – learn

f) they – teach g) it – bring h) you – take

## Aufgabe 2: She hasn't arrived

**Verwende noch einmal die Sätze aus Aufgabe 1 und verneine sie.**

Beispiel: a) *She hasn't arrived.*

## Aufgabe 3: Cleaning the house

**Heute hat Familie Singasong gemeinsam Großputz gemacht. Einiges ist schon geschafft, anderes muss noch erledigt werden. Setze die Verben in Klammern ins *present perfect*.**

a) Tim ______________________________ (tidy) his bedroom, but he ______________________________ (not tidy) the living-room yet.

b) Suzy and her father ______________________________ (take) the empty glass bottles to the container, but they ______________________________ (not take) the empty tins there yet.

c) Suzy ______________________________ (clean) the kitchen windows, but she ______________________________ (not clean) the kitchen floor yet.

d) Mrs Singasong ______________________________ (throw) away some broken cups, but she ______________________________ (throw) away the broken plates yet.

e) Tim and his mother ______________________________ (put) the old toys into boxes, but they ______________________________ (not put) the old picture books into boxes yet.

f) Mr Singasong ______________________________ (wash) the dishes, but he ______________________________ (not wash) the clothes yet.

g) Tim and Suzy ______________________________ (dust: *abstauben, regelmäßiges Verb*) the cupboard in the living-room, but they ______________________________ (not dust) the cupboard in the hall yet.

## Aufgabe 4: Lucky and unlucky people

**Einige Mitschüler von Suzy hatten heute Pech, andere großes Glück. Suche die passenden Paare aus den angegebenen Verben heraus und setze sie im *present perfect* in die Lücken ein.**

**win/lose – find/lose – score (*ein Tor schießen; regelmäßiges Verb*)/not keep – catch/miss – exchange (*tauschen: regelmäßiges Verb*)/get**

a) Olivia is lucky! She ______________________ the bus. But Daniel ______________________ the bus, so he is late for school.

b) George is happy. He ______________________ ten pounds on the floor. But Ruby is sad because she ______________________ some money.

c) Lucas feels good. He ______________________ a game of cards. But Sophie ______________________ a computer game, so she feels bad.

d) Harry ______________________ some magic cards with his friend. He likes his new cards very much. But Abigail ______________________ a pack of magic cards from her friend that she doesn't like.

e) Lisa ______________________ a goal for her football team. She is smiling. But Will the goalkeeper (*Torwart*) is crying because he ______________________ the ball.

## 5.2 Die Satzstellung im *present perfect*

- Anders als im Deutschen steht im Englischen das *past participle* vor dem Objekt:

| | | | | | |
|---|---|---|---|---|---|
| Sue | has | **given** | me | the map. | |
| Sue | hat | | mir | die Landkarte | **gegeben**. |

- Das gilt auch für die Satzstellung in **Fragen** (siehe Kapitel 10):

| | | | | | |
|---|---|---|---|---|---|
| Has | she | **shown** | you | the picture? | |
| Hat | sie | | dir | das Bild | **gezeigt**? |

- Die **Signalwörter** *just*, *already*, *ever*, *never* stehen in Aussagesätzen und Fragen vor dem *past participle*:

| | | | | | |
|---|---|---|---|---|---|
| | I | have | **just** | seen | a good film. |
| | She | has | **never** | heard | of this shop. |
| | They | have | **already** | eaten | everything. |
| Have | you | | **ever** | met | her? |

- Mit *not … yet* drückt man aus, dass etwas noch nicht geschehen ist. Das Signalwort *yet* steht hierbei am Satzende:

  He hasn't cleaned the kitchen **yet**.

### Aufgabe 5: What have they given each other?

**Bringe die Wörter in die richtige Reihenfolge.**

a) given – Tim – a bowl of milk – has – Lily

________________________________________

b) her son – a sandwich – made – Mrs Singasong – has

________________________________________

c) Suzy – brought – her father – has – the newspaper

________________________________________

d) Lily – carried – a ball – has – to Suzy

________________________________________

e) her husband – has – Mrs Singasong – shown – a pair of shoes

________________________________________

## Aufgabe 6: Things you have never done

**Formuliere Fragen mit *ever* und Antworten mit *never* im *present perfect.***

Beispiel: a) be at the North Pole (*Nordpol*):

*Have you ever been at the North Pole?*

*No, I have never been at the North Pole.*

b) sleep in an igloo (*Iglu*)

________________________________________

________________________________________

c) spend a whole day in the dark

________________________________________

________________________________________

d) eat raw (*roh*) fish

________________________________________

________________________________________

e) ride a dog sledge (*Hundeschlitten*)

________________________________________

________________________________________

f) walk on an iceberg

________________________________________

________________________________________

## Aufgabe 7: Organizing a school trip

**Die Schüler aus Tims Klasse organisieren einen Theaterbesuch. Formuliere Fragen mit *already* und Antworten mit *not yet* im *present perfect*.**

a) choose a play – *Have you already chosen a play?*
*No, I haven't chosen a play yet.*

b) buy the theatre tickets

________________________________________

________________________________________

c) organize (*organisieren, regelmäßiges Verb*) a bus

________________________________________

________________________________________

d) count the pupils in our tutor group

________________________________________

________________________________________

e) ask the headmaster for permission (*Erlaubnis*)

________________________________________

________________________________________

f) write a letter with information for the parents

________________________________________

________________________________________

g) find any teachers who want to come with us

________________________________________

________________________________________

## 5.3 Der Gebrauch von *present perfect* und *simple past*

**In diesen Fällen verwendest du das *present perfect:***

- Wenn Handlungen in der Vergangenheit stattfanden, ihr Ergebnis oder ihre Auswirkung aber in der Gegenwart spürbar ist:

  I **have broken** my arm.
  → Der Arm ist jetzt eingegipst, tut vielleicht noch weh.

  I **have lost** John's phone number.
  → Ich kann John nicht anrufen.

- Wenn Handlungen gerade erst abgeschlossen wurden:

  She **has just arrived**.

  **Signalwort**: *just*

- Wenn du über einen Zeitraum sprichst, der bis in die Gegenwart reicht:

  I **have never been** to China.
  He **has already started** to learn English.

  **Signalwörter**: *already, ever, never, so far*

**In diesen Fällen verwendest du das *simple past:***

- Wenn du über abgeschlossene Handlungen in der Vergangenheit sprichst. Häufig nennst du gleichzeitig einen bestimmten Zeitpunkt in der Vergangenheit.

  They **went** to Scotland last year.
  I **loved** this band when I was young.

  **Signalwörter**: *yesterday, last week, last year, in the morning, in the evening; when* (zur Einleitung von Nebensätzen)

**Achtung**: Das deutsche Perfekt musst du häufig als *simple past* übersetzen:

Ich habe ihn gestern getroffen.
I **met** him yesterday. (Signalwort!)

## Aufgabe 8: Bobby Brilliant

**Ergänze den Text über den Sänger Bobby Brilliant, einen von Suzys Lieblingssängern, mit den angegebenen Verbformen.**

**was – have been – have had – told – thought – have decided – started – met – have had – performed – have just had – was**

Hi, I am Bobby Brilliant. I (a) ______________________

a singer all my life. I (b) ______________________ to sing

when I (c) ______________________ a small child. At five I

(d) ______________________ in a TV show for the first time.

Since then I (e) ______________________ many number one hits.

I (f) ______________________ the other singers of my boy group

three years ago. Of course, we (g) ______________________

good times and bad times together since then. Two months ago I

(h) ______________________ about finishing our band project

and starting to sing solo again. But our manager

(i) ______________________ us that we should stay together.

And he (j) ______________________ right. We

(k) ______________________ another number one hit. So we

(l) ______________________ to record our next album soon.

## Aufgabe 9: German fans

**Bobby Brilliant hat viele Fans in Deutschland, die ihm Mails schreiben. Heute beantwortet er ihre Fragen. Entscheide, ob du die Ausdrücke in den Klammern ins *simple past* oder ins *present perfect* setzen musst.**

a) "_______________ (ever be) to Germany, Bobby?"

b) "Yes, I _______________ (travel) to Germany many times. Last year I _______________ (go) to Berlin to visit some friends, for example."

c) "_______________ (ever try) German food, Bobby?"

d) "Yes, I once _______________ (eat) a schnitzel and I _______________ (like) it a lot."

e) "_______________ (ever learn) German, Bobby?"

f) "Yes, I _______________ (have) two years of German at school, but I _______________ (already forget) everything."

g) "_______________ (already decide) about the title of your next album?"

h) "Well, I _______________ (not talk) about it with the other band members yet. But I _______________ (just have) a brilliant idea for a new song called 'Too many questions'."

## Aufgabe 10: Learning English

**Übersetze die Sätze ins Englische.**

a) Letztes Jahr haben wir einige Klassenarbeiten in Englisch geschrieben.

______________________________________________

______________________________________________

b) Ich habe schon viele Übungen in diesem Buch gemacht.

______________________________________________

c) So viele englische Sätze habe ich noch nie gelesen.

______________________________________________

d) Heute Morgen hatten wir in der Schule Englisch.

______________________________________________

e) Gerade habe ich diese Übung beendet.

______________________________________________

# Abschlusstest online

# 5

Toll! Du hast das **Kapitel 5 – Das *present perfect*** durchgearbeitet. Dabei hast du noch einmal gelernt, warum es im Englischen so viele Vergangenheitsformen gibt: weil man damit ganz unterschiedliche Dinge ausdrücken kann. Mit dem *present perfect* sprichst du über Dinge, die gerade erst passiert sind und deren Auswirkungen noch spürbar sind.

**So funktioniert der Abschlusstest online:**
Um deinen Lernerfolg zu überprüfen, kannst du nun die Abschlusstests machen. Gehe auf
**https://www.klett-lerntraining.de/9Y2A**
und wähle das Kapitel und einen Test aus.

Welche Tests es gibt, siehst du unten in der Tabelle. Nach jedem Test bekommst du eine Auswertung.

Willst du immer im Blick haben, welche Themen du schon kannst oder was du besser wiederholen solltest? Dann schreibe deine Ergebnisse in die Tabelle.

## Mein Ergebnis im Abschlusstest online – Kapitel 5

| Thema | Mein Ergebnis |
|---|---|
| Bejahte und verneinte Formen im *present perfect* | |
| Die Satzstellung im *present perfect* | |
| Der Gebrauch von *present perfect* und *simple past* | |

# 6 Zukunftsformen

## 6.1 *Going to-future*

### Bildung des *going to-future*

Um einen Plan für die nahe Zukunft zu beschreiben, kannst du das ***going to-future*** verwenden. Diese Form wird so gebildet:

***am/is/are* + *going to* + Infinitiv**

Zur Verneinung setzt du ***not*** nach ***am/is/are*** ein.

| | | | | | |
|---|---|---|---|---|---|
| Singular | I | **am** | | | |
| | you | **are** | | | |
| | he/she/it | **is** | **(not)** | **going to** | sleep. |
| Plural | we | **are** | | | |
| | you | **are** | | | |
| | they | **are** | | | |

Du kannst in bejahten und verneinten Sätzen auch die entsprechenden **Kurzformen** verwenden:

I'**m** going to buy some chocolate.
I'**m not** going to buy cheese.

He'**s** going to visit his friend.
He **isn't** going to visit his aunt.

## Aufgabe 1: You are going to begin

**Bilde bejahte Sätze im *going to-future*.**

a) you – begin the exercise: *You are going to begin the exercise.*

b) I – write down a sentence ____________________

c) he – explain the *going to-future* ____________________

d) we – learn the rules ____________________

e) they – choose the right form ____________________

f) she – think of the answer ____________________

## Aufgabe 2: A busy family

**Was haben die Singasongs für Pläne? Schreibe Sätze mit dem *going to-future*.**

a) Suzy: go to hairdresser – not buy new T-shirt
*Suzy is going to go to the hairdresser.*
*She is not going to buy a new T-shirt.*

b) Tim: watch volleyball match – not got to cinema with Nat

____________________

____________________

c) Mr and Mrs Singasong: play tennis – not have tea with their neighbours

____________________

____________________

d) Tim: give concert with school orchestra – not work in the garden

____________________

____________________

e) Mr and Mrs Singasong: buy vegetables at market – go swimming

____________________

____________________

## 6.2 *Will-future*

Mit dem ***will-future*** kannst du über Zukünftiges sprechen. Du verwendest es, wenn du Vermutungen über die Zukunft äußern willst oder über zukünftige Ereignisse sprichst, die du nicht beeinflussen kannst.

### Bejahte Form des *will-future*

Das ***will-future*** bildest du so:

***will*** **+ Infinitiv des Verbs**

Das ***will-future*** lautet für alle Personen gleich.

| | | | |
|---|---|---|---|
| Singular | I | | |
| | you | | |
| | he/she/it | **will** | **come** |
| Plural | we | | |
| | you | | |
| | they | | |

Neben der Langform ***will*** kannst du auch die Kurzform ***'ll*** verwenden:

I'**ll** come. He'**ll** come. They'**ll** come.

### Verneinte Form

Zur Verneinung setzt du ***not*** nach ***will*** ein:

| | | | | |
|---|---|---|---|---|
| Singular | I | | | |
| | you | | | |
| | he/she/it | **will** | **not** | **come**. |
| Plural | we | | | |
| | you | | | |
| | they | | | |

Die Kurzform von ***will not*** lautet ***won't***:

You **won't** come. She **won't** come. We **won't** come.

## Aufgabe 3: Dreams of the future

**Wie sieht wohl die Zukunft aus? Bilde Sätze mit dem *will-future* und schreibe sie auf.**

a) I – have lots of money – not be poor
   *I will have lots of money. I won't be poor.*

b) you – own a big car – not use the bus

c) he – sell many CDs – not be an unknown (*unbekannt*) singer

d) she – play in a film – not do silly jobs

e) we – travel a lot – not stay at home

f) they – have a lot of friends – not feel lonely (*einsam*)

## Aufgabe 4: A family in the year 2050

**Vielleicht hat im Jahr 2050 jede Familie ihren Hausroboter? Bringe die Buchstaben der Verben in die richtige Reihenfolge und setze diese in das *will-future*.**

a) At six o'clock the robot ______________________ (ekwa) up the family.

b) Then it ______________________ (ekma) coffee, tea and toast.

c) Next it ______________________ (tkea) the clothes out of the cupboard.

d) It ______________________ (hple) everybody to dress.

e) Later it ______________________ (og) to the supermarket.

f) It ______________________ (uby) food for an excellent lunch.

## Aufgabe 5: No robots in the year 2050

**Verwende noch einmal die Sätze aus Aufgabe 4 und schreibe sie in verneinter Form auf.**

## 6.3 Der Gebrauch von *going to-future* und *will-future*

### In diesen Fällen verwendest du das *going to-future:*

- Wenn du einen **Plan** oder eine bestimmte **Absicht** hast:

  I'**m going to visit** my friend tonight.

- Wenn du über **absehbare Ereignisse** der nahen Zukunft sprichst, für die es bereits Vorzeichen gibt:

  Look at this traffic! We **are going to be** late for the concert.
  → Aufgrund des starken Verkehrs ist es wahrscheinlich, dass die Autofahrt länger dauert als geplant.

  There is nothing in the fridge. We are **going to stay hungry** tonight.
  → Der leere Kühlschrank zeigt an, dass das Abendessen ausfällt.

### In diesen Fällen verwendest du das *will-future*:

- Wenn du über **Ereignisse** in der **Zukunft** sprichst, die du **nicht selbst beeinflussen** kannst, sondern die von **äußeren Umständen** abhängen:

  The weather **will be** fine tomorrow.

- Wenn du **Vermutungen** über die **Zukunft** ausdrückst:

  **I think** the English football team **will lose**.

  **Signalwörter**: *I think, I promise, I hope, I'm sure, probably*

### Unterschiede zur deutschen Zeitenverwendung

Das deutsche **Präsens** musst du im Englischen oft mit dem ***going to-future*** oder ***will-future*** übersetzen.

| | |
|---|---|
| Ich **treffe** morgen Sue. | I'**m going to meet** Sue tomorrow. |
| Morgen **scheint** die Sonne. | The sun **will shine** tomorrow. |

## Aufgabe 6: Bobby Brilliant and the future

**Bobby Brilliant, Suzys Lieblingssänger, wird von einer Zeitschrift interviewt. Setze die unten stehenden Verbformen in die Lücken ein.**

**are you going to give – will see – am going to work – am going to give – will be – am not going to tell – will be – are you going to do – won't be**

a) „What ______________________________ tonight, Bobby?"

b) "I ______________________________ two more interviews, one for a radio station and one for a youth magazine. So I hope your interview ______________________________ very long."

c) "______________________________ any live concerts this summer, Bobby?"

d) "I think there ______________________________ three open air concerts in July. But in the next few weeks I ______________________________ on some new songs."

e) "I'm sure there ______________________________ some new special effects in your show?"

f) "I promise that my fans ______________________________ a very good show. But I ______________________________ you more, it's all a big secret!"

## Aufgabe 7: A barbecue at school

**Suzys Klasse plant eine große Grillfeier mit Schülern, Eltern und Lehrern. Entscheide, ob du die Verben in Klammern ins *going to-future* oder ins *will-future* setzen musst.**

a) Daniel: "I hope the weather ____________________ (be) fine on Saturday."

b) Ruby: "I hope so, too. I ____________________ (watch) the weather report tonight."

c) Lucas: "What about Suzy and her parents, ____________________ (come) to our barbecue party?"

d) Sophie: "I'm sure Suzy ____________________ (come), but I don't know about her parents' plans."

e) Lisa: "____________________ (make) your famous chocolate cake for the barbecue, Harry?"

f) Harry: "No, I ____________________ (bring) a potato salad to the party."

g) Lisa: "Oh, what a pity (*wie schade*). I hope someone else ____________________ (make) a nice dessert."

h) Lucas: "Daniel ____________________ (be) our DJ from 6 o'clock till 8 o'clock, but what about the rest of the time?"

i) Ruby: "I ____________________ (ask) Will."

j) Lucas: "Yes, that's a good idea, I think he ____________________ (say) yes."

# Abschlusstest online 6

Großartig! Du hast das **Kapitel 6 – Zukunftsformen** durchgearbeitet. Dabei hast du wiederholt, dass du im Englischen mehrere Möglichkeiten hast, über die Zukunft zu sprechen: mit dem *going to-future* beispielsweise über Pläne, mit dem *will-future* über Dinge, die du nicht beeinflussen kannst.

**So funktioniert der Abschlusstest online:**
Um deinen Lernerfolg zu überprüfen, kannst du nun die Abschlusstests machen. Gehe auf
**https://www.klett-lerntraining.de/9Y2A**
und wähle das Kapitel und einen Test aus.

Welche Tests es gibt, siehst du unten in der Tabelle. Nach jedem Test bekommst du eine Auswertung.

Willst du immer im Blick haben, welche Themen du schon kannst oder was du besser wiederholen solltest? Dann schreibe deine Ergebnisse in die Tabelle.

## Mein Ergebnis im Abschlusstest online – Kapitel 6

| Thema | Mein Ergebnis |
|---|---|
| *Going to-future* | |
| *Will-future* | |
| Der Gebrauch von *going to-future* und *will-future* | |

# 7 Die modalen Hilfsverben

## 7.1 *Can/can't*

Das Hilfsverb ***can*** drückt aus, dass du etwas tun **kannst** oder **darfst**. Hilfsverben können immer nur zusammen mit einem Vollverb gebraucht werden; sie stehen nie allein im Satz.

Die Form ***can*** lautet für alle Personen gleich. Sie steht immer zusammen mit dem Infinitiv des Vollverbs:

| | | | |
|---|---|---|---|
| Singular | I | | |
| | you | | |
| | he/she/it | **can** | play |
| Plural | we | | |
| | you | | |
| | they | | |

Die verneinte Form von ***can*** heißt in der Langform ***cannot***, in der Kurzform ***can't***.

Du kannst ***can*** auch verwenden, um höfliche Aufforderungen in Form einer Frage zu formulieren:

**Can** you give me the key, please?

**Achtung**: Anders als das deutsche „kann" darf ***can*** nie alleine stehen!

Ich **kann** Englisch. I **can speak** English.

Im Deutschen steht das **Vollverb** am Satzende, im Englischen **direkt nach *can***:

| | | | |
|---|---|---|---|
| We | can | **write** | a mail. |
| Wir | können | eine Mail | **schreiben**. |

## Aufgabe 1: Things you can do

**Was kannst du alles und was nicht? Beginne deine Sätze mit *I can* oder *I can't*.**

a) sing an English rap song ______________________________

b) bark like a dog ______________________________

c) write with my toes (*Zehen*) ______________________________

d) do a somersault (*Purzelbaum*) ______________________________

e) walk on my hands ______________________________

f) spell my name backwards ______________________________

g) do a magic trick ______________________________

h) sleep a whole weekend ______________________________

## Aufgabe 2: Things your friend can do

**Verwende noch einmal die Sätze aus Aufgabe 1. Sprich nun über deinen Freund/deine Freundin oder deinen Bruder/deine Schwester und schreibe die Sätze auf.**

## Aufgabe 3: Classroom phrases

**Im Unterricht kommen täglich jede Menge Anweisungen vor. Bilde mit den angegebenen Bausteinen mindestens acht sinnvolle Sätze mit *can*.**

Beispiel: a) *Can you switch on the light, please?*

| | |
|---|---|
| ~~switch on~~ | the board |
| repeat | your books |
| take out | your pens |
| close | the windows |
| clean | the classroom |
| write down | the phrase |
| tidy up | ~~the light~~ |
| open | these words |

## 7.2 *Must, needn't* und *mustn't*

### Das modale Hilfsverb *must*

***Must*** ist ein Hilfsverb, benötigt also im Satz immer zusätzlich ein Vollverb. Du drückst damit aus, dass jemand etwas tun **muss**.

Die Form ***must*** ist für alle Personen gleich. Sie wird zusammen mit dem **Infinitiv des Vollverbs** verwendet.

She **must** work every day.

### *Needn't* als Verneinung von *must*

Als **Verneinung** von *must* wird ***needn't*** (Langform *need not*) verwendet. Du drückst damit also aus, dass jemand etwas **nicht tun muss** oder **nicht zu tun braucht**.

Auch die Form ***needn't*** ist für alle Personen gleich und steht direkt vor dem **Infinitiv des Vollverbs**.

You **needn't** clean the kitchen.

### Die Verwendung von *mustn't*

***Mustn't*** drückt aus, dass jemand etwas nicht tun **darf**. Auch von diesem Hilfsverb gibt es nur eine Form für alle Personen, und es steht vor dem Infinitiv des Vollverbs:

You **mustn't** take this knife.

**Achtung Verwechslungsgefahr:**

| | |
|---|---|
| Er **muss nicht** lernen. | He **needn't** learn. |
| Er **darf nicht** rennen. | He **mustn't** run. |

## Aufgabe 4: Rules for Suzy and Tim

**Suzy und Tim haben mit ihren Eltern ein paar Regeln vereinbart. Schreibe sie in der richtigen Reihenfolge auf.**

a) must – they – polite – to their parents – be

________________________________________

b) where they go – their parents – they – tell – must

________________________________________

c) before 8 pm – come home – must – they

________________________________________

d) do their homework – must – every day – they

________________________________________

e) talk about – they – problems at school – must

________________________________________

f) they – with the housework – help – must – once a day

________________________________________

g) must – they – for their mobile phones – pay – with their pocket money

________________________________________

h) introduce (*vorstellen*) – to their parents – they – their friends – must

________________________________________

## Aufgabe 5: Rules for Mr and Mrs Singasong

**Suzy und Tim haben auch Verhaltensregeln für ihre Eltern aufgestellt. Formuliere diese Liste in Sätze mit *must not*/*mustn't* um. Beginne jeweils mit "Mr und Mrs Singasong ..." oder einfach mit "They ...".**

a) Do not read our diaries.

*They must not read Tim's and Suzy's diaries.*

b) Do not control our mails.

___

c) Do not throw away any of our clothes.

___

d) Do not tidy up our rooms.

___

e) Do not look into our school bags.

___

f) Do not tell us what to eat.

___

g) Do not enter our rooms without asking.

___

h) Do not turn off our music.

___

## Aufgabe 6: What Tim and Suzy needn't do

**Tim und Suzy haben einige Pflichten, es gibt aber auch Dinge, um die sie sich nicht kümmern müssen. Drücke dies mit dem Hilfsverb *needn't* aus.**

a) Tim and Suzy – make the sandwiches for their school lunch

*Tim and Suzy needn't make the sandwiches for their school lunch.*

b) Suzy – mow the lawn (*Rasen mähen*)

______________________________________________

______________________________________________

c) Tim – repair his bike

______________________________________________

______________________________________________

d) Tim and Suzy – iron (*bügeln*) their clothes

______________________________________________

______________________________________________

e) Suzy – bake tea cakes

______________________________________________

______________________________________________

f) Tim and Suzy – do the shopping

______________________________________________

______________________________________________

g) Suzy – wash the car

______________________________________________

______________________________________________

h) Tim – clean Lily's basket

______________________________________________

______________________________________________

## Aufgabe 7: In the restaurant

**Die Familie Singasong geht zu besonderen Gelegenheiten oft zum Essen in ein Restaurant. Dort ist manches anders als zu Hause. Bilde acht sinnvolle Sätze mit den angegebenen Bausteinen und schreibe sie auf.**

| | | |
|---|---|---|
| | | do the cooking. |
| | | smoke. |
| | can | wash the dishes. |
| They | must | pay the bill. |
| | needn't | talk to the other guests. |
| | mustn't | put their feet on the table. |
| | | bring their own sandwiches. |
| | | order something to drink. |

________________________________________

________________________________________

________________________________________

________________________________________

________________________________________

________________________________________

________________________________________

________________________________________

## Aufgabe 8: Schools and rules

**Sicher kennst du die folgenden Verhaltensregeln aus deiner eigenen Schule. Vervollständige die Sätze jeweils mit der englischen Entsprechung des in Klammern angegebenen Hilfsverbs.**

a) Pupils ______________________ (*nicht müssen*) sit on the floor.

b) But they ______________________ (*nicht dürfen*) throw rubbish on the floor.

c) Teachers ______________________ (*dürfen*) control the pupils' homework.

d) But they ______________________ (*nicht müssen*) do the homework for their pupils.

e) Pupils ______________________ (*können*) have a break between lessons.

f) But they ______________________ (*nicht dürfen*) sleep during lessons.

g) Pupils ______________________ (*müssen*) respect each other (*gegenseitig*).

h) But they ______________________ (*nicht müssen*) love each other.

i) Parents ______________________ (*können*) help their children with their homework.

j) But they ______________________ (*nicht können*) write the school tests for their children.

## 7.3 *Could, may, shall*

### Das modale Hilfsverb *could*

Das modale Hilfsverb ***could*** (könnte) wird wie alle Hilfsverben zusammen mit dem **Infinitiv des Vollverbs** verwendet und hat nur eine Form für alle Personen. Man kann damit:

- über **Möglichkeiten** sprechen:

  It **could** snow tomorrow.

- etwas **anbieten**:

  I **could** help you with the dishes.

- eine **Bitte** äußern:

  **Could** you fetch the newspaper, please?

### Das modale Hilfsverb *may*

Auch nach dem Hilfsverb ***may*** (dürfen) steht immer der Infinitiv des Vollverbs. Du kannst damit sehr höfliche, förmliche Bitten äußern:

**May** I get a cup of tea, please?

### Das modale Hilfsverb *shall*

Mit ***shall*** (sollen) kannst du **Vorschläge** bzw. **Angebote** machen.
Beachte, dass du ***shall*** nur in der 1. Person (Singular und Plural) verwendest, also mit *I* oder *we*:

**Shall** I walk the dog?

## Aufgabe 9: At the hotel reception

**Du unternimmst mit deiner Familie eine Reise nach London. Dort wohnt ihr in einem Hotel. Da du als Einzige(r) Englisch kannst, wirst du mit vielen Fragen an die Rezeption geschickt. Setze *could*, *may* oder *shall* ein.**

a) ___________ you give us a map of the city centre, please?

b) Where ___________ we put our keys when we leave the hotel?

c) ___________ I get a bottle of water for my mother, please?

d) ___________ somebody bring us fresh towels (*Handtücher*), please?

e) When ___________ we pay the hotel bill?

f) ___________ my father make a phone call, please?

g) ___________ I write down our German address for you?

h) ___________ we put our passports (*Pässe*) into the hotel safe, please?

## Aufgabe 10: More questions at the hotel

**Formuliere jetzt selbstständig Fragen, die du an der Rezeption des Hotels stellen kannst. Die Situationen sind vorgegeben, den genauen Wortlaut der Frage musst du dir aber jeweils selbst überlegen.**

a) It is very cold in your hotel room.

   *Could you turn on the heating in our room, please?*

b) The TV in your hotel room doesn't work.

c) You want to eat some ice-cream.

d) Your mother wants to change a twenty pound note.

e) Your father offers (*anbieten*) to carry your bags to the hotel room.

f) Your mother wants to sit down on a sofa in the hotel lobby (*Eingangshalle*).

## Aufgabe 11: Tim's school trip

**Tim bereitet sich gerade auf einen mehrtägigen Schulausflug nach Brighton vor. Im Gespräch mit seinen Eltern ist jeweils nur eines der angegebenen modalen Hilfsverben passend. Streiche das unpassende Modalverb durch.**

a) Tim: "*Shall/Must* I take my boots or my trainers with me? What do you think, Mum?"

b) Mum: "Well, you *can/mustn't* pack both into your suitcase (*Koffer*), Tim. It is big enough for both."

c) Dad: "But remember that you *must/needn't* carry your suitcase all the way to the bus station, so do not put too much into it!"

d) Tim: "All right, Dad. *Shall/May* I borrow your new windbreaker (*Windjacke*) then? It is very light, isn't it?"

e) Dad: "Okay, Tim, but you *must/could* remember that it is not only a very light but also a very expensive jacket."

f) Tim: "I know that, Dad. You *mustn't/needn't* worry."

g) Mum: "And Tim, you *mustn't/must* forget your mobile."

h) Tim: "How *shall/could* I forget my mobile? It's already in my bag."

i) Mum: "Good, *could/may* you then call us every day, please?"

j) Tim: "Oh Mum, I really *can/cannot* do that. But I *can/needn't* send you a short text message instead (*stattdessen*)."

k) Mum: "Well, is there anything else we *must/can* do for you?"

l) Tim: "Yes Mum, you and Dad *cannot/mustn't* give me any more tips for the trip ..."

# Abschlusstest online 7

Glückwunsch! Du hast das **Kapitel 7 – Die modalen Hilfsverben** durchgearbeitet. Dabei hast du gelernt, wie man müssen, dürfen, können im Englischen ausdrückt – und dass es dabei falsche Freunde zu beachten gilt!

**So funktioniert der Abschlusstest online:**
Um deinen Lernerfolg zu überprüfen, kannst du nun die Abschlusstests machen.
Gehe auf
**https://www.klett-lerntraining.de/9Y2A**
und wähle das Kapitel und einen Test aus.

Welche Tests es gibt, siehst du unten in der Tabelle. Nach jedem Test bekommst du eine Auswertung.

Willst du immer im Blick haben, welche Themen du schon kannst oder was du besser wiederholen solltest? Dann schreibe deine Ergebnisse in die Tabelle.

## Mein Ergebnis im Abschlusstest online – Kapitel 7

| Thema | Mein Ergebnis |
|---|---|
| *Can/can't* | |
| *Must, needn't, mustn't* | |
| *Could, may, shall* | |

# 8 Adjektive

## 8.1 Gebrauch und Steigerung von Adjektiven

Adjektive beschreiben die **Eigenschaften** von Personen oder Dingen. Sie stehen direkt **vor dem Nomen** oder **nach *to be*** (und einigen anderen Verben):

I am playing an **exciting** game.
This game is **exciting**.

### Steigerung mit -er/-est

Man steigert Adjektive, um Vergleiche anstellen zu können. Die Steigerung mit **-er/-est** wird verwendet für:

- einsilbige Adjektive
- zweisilbige Adjektive, die auf **y**, **er** und **le** enden

| **Grundform** (basic form) | **Komparativ** (comparative) | **Superlativ** (superlative) |
|---|---|---|
| old<br>fast | old + **er** → old**er**<br>fast + **er** → fast**er** | old + est → the old**est**<br>fast + est → the fast**est** |
| happy<br>clever<br>simple | happy + **er** → happi**er**<br>clever + **er** → clever**er**<br>simple + **er** → simpl**er** | happy + **est** → the happi**est**<br>clever + **est** → the clever**est**<br>simple + **est** → the simpl**est** |

**Beachte folgende Regeln bei der Schreibung:**

- Bei einsilbigen Adjektiven wird der **Endkonsonant nach einem Kurzvokal** verdoppelt:

| | | |
|---|---|---|
| bi**g** | bi**gg**er | the bi**gg**est |

- Ein stummes **e** am Wortende fällt weg:

| | | |
|---|---|---|
| strang**e** | stranger | the strangest |
| simpl**e** | simpler | the simplest |

- Am Wortende von zweisilbigen Adjektiven wird **y** zu **i**:

| | | |
|---|---|---|
| scar**y** | scar**i**er | the scar**i**est |

## Steigerung mit *more/most*

Die Steigerung mit ***more/most*** wird verwendet für:

- zweisilbige Adjektive, die nicht auf **y**, **er** oder **le** enden
- mehrsilbige Adjektive

| Grundform | Komparativ | Superlativ |
|---|---|---|
| boring | **more** boring | **the most** boring |
| beautiful | **more** beautiful | **the most** beautiful |

## Unregelmäßige Steigerungsformen

| Grundform | Komparativ | Superlativ |
|---|---|---|
| good | **better** | **the best** |
| bad | **worse** | **the worst** |

## Aufgabe 1: A lot of adjectives

**Bei diesen Sätzen sind die Buchstaben der Adjektive durcheinandergeraten. Wie heißen diese Wörter richtig? Tipp: In jedem Satzpaar geht es um einen Gegensatz!**

a) Does the film have a ______________________ (paphy) ending?

No, the ending is ______________________ (dab).

b) Is the water ______________________ (arwm) enough to go swimming?

No, the water is too ______________________ (cldo).

c) Is this the ______________________ (tighr) answer?

No, the answer is ______________________ (ronwg).

d) Is the bottle still ______________________ (lulf)?

No, the bottle is already ______________________ (metyp).

e) Do you have a ______________________ (satf) car?

No, my car is ______________________ (wols).

f) Is this a ______________________ (iffidltuc) exercise?

No, the exercise is ______________________ (aeys).

## Aufgabe 2: Nothing to wear

**Suzy und Tim finden, sie haben nichts anzuziehen! Schreibe Sätze mit passenden Adjektiven im Komparativ (der ersten Steigerungsform), die ausdrücken, was Suzy und Tim ihrer Meinung nach brauchen.**

a) Tim: "These jeans are too short." – I need longer jeans.

b) Suzy: "This jumper is much too big."

c) Tim: "This T-shirt is too boring."

d) Suzy: "These shoes are too dirty."

e) Tim: "This jacket is too long."

f) Suzy: "These trousers are too small."

## Aufgabe 3: Holidays in Scotland

**Schottland hat eine Menge Rekorde zu bieten. Setze die vorgegebenen Adjektive in ihrer Superlativform in die Lücken ein.**

a) The ______________________________ (high) mountain of Scotland is called Ben Nevis.

b) Ben Nevis is also the ______________________________ (cold) place in Scotland.

c) The ______________________________ (wet) area of Scotland are the Western Highlands.

d) One of the ______________________________ (sunny) cities is Aberdeen.

e) Loch Ness is one of the ______________________________ (deep) Scottish lakes.

f) The ______________________________ (interesting) tale (*Geschichte*) is about Nessie, the monster of Loch Ness.

g) You can visit the ______________________________ (big) city of Scotland, Glasgow.

h) Try the ______________________________ (good) Scottish biscuits, the butter fingers.

i) Some people think that haggis (*Gericht aus Schafsinnereien*) is one of the ______________________________ (bad) things you can eat in Scotland.

j) For some tourists, the Scottish accent is the ______________________ ______________________________ (difficult) to understand.

## 8.2 Der Vergleich im Satz

Mithilfe von Adjektiven lassen sich Personen und Dinge vergleichen.

So drückst du aus, dass **etwas gleich ist**:

- ***as*** + Adjektiv in der Grundform + ***as***

  Suzy is **as old as** Laura.
  French is **as difficult as** Italian.

So drückst du aus, dass **etwas ungleich ist**:

- Adjektiv im Komparativ + ***than***

  Tim is **older than** Suzy.
  Chinese is **more difficult than** English.

- ***not as*** + Adjektiv in der Grundform + ***as***

  Suzy is **not as old as** Tim.
  English is **not as difficult as** Chinese.

### Aufgabe 4: Comparing food

**Hier gibt es einiges zu essen und zu trinken. Vergleiche mit jeweils zwei Sätzen.**

a) lemonade/mineral water (sweet)
*Lemonade is sweeter than mineral water.*
*Mineral water is not as sweet as lemonade.*

b) chocolate/apples (healthy)

______________________________

c) a pumpkin (*Kürbis*)/a tomato (small)

______________________________

d) coffee/a banana milkshake (bitter)

______________________________

e) bread/yoghurt (dry)

_______________________________________________

f) carrots/chilies (hot: *scharf*)

_______________________________________________

g) a nut/a muffin (soft)

_______________________________________________

## Aufgabe 5: Going to the cinema

**Suzy und Tim wollen ins Kino gehen. Drei Filme stehen zur Auswahl. Vergleiche diese anhand der Filmplakate und der Adjektive.**

| | | | |
|---|---|---|---|
| a) sad | b) romantic | c) short | d) exciting |
| e) scary | f) funny | g) boring | |

Beispiel: a) *"Crazy Love" is (not) as sad as "Vampire nights". But it is sadder than "Guns and horses".*

## 8.3 Mengenangaben mit *much/many/a lot of/a little/a few*

Die Wörter ***much***, ***many***, ***a lot of***, ***lots of***, ***a little***, ***a few*** bezeichnen eine unbestimmte Menge. Sie stehen vor Nomen und sagen aus, wie viel oder wenig von etwas vorhanden ist.

| | **Nichtzählbare Nomen im Singular** | **Zählbare Nomen im Plural** |
|---|---|---|
| Fragen | **much** (viel)<br>How **much** sugar do we need? | **many** (viele)<br>How **many** eggs do we need? |
| Bejahte Aussagen | **a lot of/lots of** (viel)<br>We need **a lot of/lots of** sugar.<br>**a little** (ein wenig)<br>We need **a little** sugar. | **a lot of/lots of** (viele)<br>We need **a lot of/lots of** eggs.<br>**a few** (einige)<br>We need **a few** eggs. |
| Verneinte Aussagen | **not much** (nicht viel)<br>We have**n't** got **much** sugar. | **not many** (nicht viele)<br>We have**n't** got **many** eggs. |

## Aufgabe 6: School life

**Setze *much* oder *many* ein.**

a) ________________ homework  b) ________________ pupils

c) ________________ books  d) ________________ pencils

e) ________________ exercises  f) ________________ grammar

g) ________________ tables  h) ________________ bags

i) ________________ paper  j) ________________ tests

k) ________________ questions  l) ________________ information

## Aufgabe 7: Chocolate muffins

**In der Wörterschlange sind acht Zutaten versteckt, die du für Schokoladenmuffins brauchst. Schreibe sie in die Liste und setze jeweils *a little* oder *a few* davor.**

aseggserbutterturs ugarpoiflourklömilkmnbraisinsdasschocolatewernuts

a) ______________________  b) ______________________

c) ______________________  d) ______________________

e) ______________________  f) ______________________

g) ______________________  h) ______________________

## Aufgabe 8: At the school cafeteria

**Tim und Suzy unterhalten sich in der Schulkantine mit Mrs Greta Goodfood, die dort das Essen ausgibt. Streiche im folgenden Dialog jeweils die unpassende Mengenangabe durch.**

a) Mrs Goodfood: "How *much/many* potatoes would you like?"

b) Tim: "Oh, just *a little/a few* potatoes, please. I have already eaten *a lot of/a little* salad, so I don't feel very hungry now."

c) Mrs Goodfood: "What about you, dear? How *much/many* meat balls can I give you?"

d) Suzy: "I would like just *a few/a little* meat balls, please, but maybe I could get *many/a lot of* chocolate cake for dessert?"

e) Mrs Goodfood: "How *much/many* tea do you want? A cup or a pot (*Kanne*)?"

f) Tim: "I only need a cup, thank you. I always put *much/many* milk and *a few/a little* sugar into my tea."

g) Suzy: "How *much/many* days do you work here, Mrs Goodfood?"

h) Mrs Goodfood: "I work only on *a little/a few* days per month. I don't earn *much/many* money here, so I have another job in the little café down the road."

# Abschlusstest online 8

Super! Du hast das **Kapitel 8 – Adjektive** durchgearbeitet. Du hast wiederholt, dass du mit Adjektiven Dinge und Personen näher beschreiben kannst und wie du Vergleiche damit anstellst. Außerdem hast du noch etwas über Mengenangaben gelernt.

**So funktioniert der Abschlusstest online:**
Um deinen Lernerfolg zu überprüfen, kannst du nun die Abschlusstests machen. Gehe auf
**https://www.klett-lerntraining.de/9Y2A**
und wähle das Kapitel und einen Test aus.

Welche Tests es gibt, siehst du unten in der Tabelle. Nach jedem Test bekommst du eine Auswertung.

Willst du immer im Blick haben, welche Themen du schon kannst oder was du besser wiederholen solltest? Dann schreibe deine Ergebnisse in die Tabelle.

## Mein Ergebnis im Abschlusstest online – Kapitel 8

| Thema | Mein Ergebnis |
|---|---|
| Adjektive | |
| Der Vergleich im Satz | |
| Mengenangaben mit *much/many/a lot of/ a little/a few* | |

# 9 Adverbien

## 9.1 Bildung und Gebrauch von Adverbien der Art und Weise

### Regelmäßige Formen von Adverbien der Art und Weise

Adverbien der Art und Weise (*adverbs of manner*) drücken aus, wie man etwas macht. Sie werden gebildet, indem man die Endung **ly** an das Adjektiv anhängt:

quick + ly → quickly

**Regeln zur Schreibung:**

- **le** nach Konsonant am Wortende des Adjektivs wird zu **ly**:

  terrib**le** + ly → terrib**ly**

- **y nach Konsonant** am Wortende des Adjektivs wird zu **i**:

  funn**y** + ly → funn**i**ly

- nach **ic** am Wortende des Adjektivs hängt man **ally** an:

  fantast**ic** + ly → fantast**ically**

### Unregelmäßige Formen von Adverbien der Art und Weise

Einige Adverbien werden unregelmäßig gebildet. Diese Formen musst du lernen.

good → well
fast → fast
hard → hard

Beachte folgenden Sonderfall:

friendly → in a friendly way

### Gebrauch von Adverb und Adjektiv im Vergleich

Im Deutschen haben Adjektiv und Adverb häufig die gleiche Form, im Englischen unterscheiden sie sich jedoch. Daher ist es wichtig, genau zu wissen, welche Wortart wofür verwendet wird (zum Gebrauch des Adjektivs siehe auch Kapitel 8.1):

- Mit dem Adjektiv beschreibst du einen Gegenstand oder eine Person. Du fragst: Wie ist etwas/jemand? Es steht vor dem Nomen (Substantiv oder Pronomen) oder beim Verb *to be*:

  She is a **good** singer. He is **angry**.

- Mit dem Adverb beschreibst du eine Handlung näher. Du fragst: Auf welche Art und Weise passiert etwas/wird etwas gemacht? Das Adverb bezieht sich auf das Verb:

  She sings **well**.

## Aufgabe 1: Pupils' wishes, teachers' wishes

**Bilde Adverbien zu den in Klammern angebebenen Adjektiven und setze diese in die Lücken ein.**

a) The pupils should talk to each other ________________ (quiet) during class, but they often talk to each other ________________ (loud).

b) They should learn the new words ________________ (good), but they often learn them ________________ (bad).

c) They should write ________________ (careful), but they often write ________________ (terrible).

d) The teachers should explain new rules ________________ (slow), but they often explain them ________________ (quick).

e) They should teach grammar ________________ (exciting), but they often teach it ________________ (boring).

## Aufgabe 2: A syllables quiz (Silbenrätsel)

**Wenn du die angegebenen Silben richtig kombinierst, kannst du sechs zweisilbige Adjektive mit der Endung -y bilden. Schreibe sie in die erste Spalte, bilde anschließend die Adverbformen und schreibe diese in die zweite Spalte.**

**hap – sy – ea – ry – ly – ang – friend – hung – py – fun – ry – ny**

| | Adjectives: | Adverbs: |
|---|---|---|
| a) | ___ | ___ |
| b) | ___ | ___ |
| c) | ___ | ___ |
| d) | ___ | ___ |
| e) | ___ | ___ |
| f) | ___ | ___ |

## Aufgabe 3: The Singasongs' talents

**Forme die unterstrichenen Satzteile mit Adjektiv in Konstruktionen mit Adverbien um. Schreibe die Sätze auf.**

a) Mr Singasong is a good cook. *Mr Singasong cooks well.*

b) Mrs Singasong is a careful driver.

c) Tim is a fantastic singer.

d) Suzy is a beautiful dancer.

e) Mrs Singasong is an aggressive *(aggressiv)* badminton player.

f) Tim is a fast swimmer.

g) Suzy is a nervous speaker.

h) Mr Singasong is an awful painter.

i) Tim is a hard worker.

j) Mrs Singasong is a nice actress.

## Aufgabe 4: Halloween

**Entscheide, ob in der Lücke ein Adjektiv oder Adverb benötigt wird.**

a) On the night of Oktober 31st many children in Britain are ____________________ (excited).

b) They dress up (*verkleiden*) as ____________________ (terrible) ghosts or monsters.

c) A ____________________ (good) costume is very important for Halloween.

d) The children go from house to house and ask ____________________ (loud) for sweets.

e) Sometimes they laugh ____________________ (spooky).

f) Sometimes they also tell ____________________ (scary) ghost stories to their neighbours.

g) The children try ____________________ (hard) to frighten everybody.

h) They shout ____________________ (angry) if they don't get any treats (*Leckereien*).

i) Many families prepare ____________________ (careful) for Halloween.

j) They decorate their houses ____________________ (nice).

k) They put ____________________ (special) pumpkins (*Kürbisse*) in front of their doors.

l) And of course there are often ____________________ (brilliant) Halloween parties.

## 9.2 Steigerung von Adverbien

Auch mit Adverbien kannst du Vergleiche anstellen. Dazu brauchst du ihre Steigerungsformen. Die Steigerung von Adverbien folgt ähnlichen Regeln wie die der Adjektive (siehe Kapitel 8.1).

### Steigerung mit -er/-est

Die Steigerung mit **-er/-est** verwendest du für einsilbige Adverbien:

| **Grundform** (basic form) | **Komparativ** (comparative) | **Superlativ** (superlative) |
|---|---|---|
| hard | hard + **er** → hard**er** | hard + est → hard**est** |

### Steigerung mit *more/most*

Die Steigerung mit **more/most** verwendest du für Adverbien, die auf **ly** enden:

| **Grundform** | **Komparativ** | **Superlativ** |
|---|---|---|
| angrily | **more** angrily | **most** angrily |
| quickly | **more** quickly | **most** quickly |

### Unregelmäßige Steigerungsformen

| **Grundform** | **Komparativ** | **Superlativ** |
|---|---|---|
| well | **better** | **best** |
| badly | **worse** | **worst** |

### Der Vergleich im Satz

Genau wie Adjektive vergleichst du auch Adverbien mit (***not***) ***as*** und ***than***:

Becky runs **as quickly as** Robert.
Jacob does not run **as quickly as** Robert.
Becky runs **more quickly than** Jacob.

## Aufgabe 5: Your talents

**Kannst du gut prahlen? Dann fällt dir die Aufgabe bestimmt leicht. Schreibe Sätze auf, in denen du Adverbien im Komparativ (der ersten Steigerungsform) verwendest, um zu sagen, was du alles besser kannst als die genannten Tiere.**

a) run – fast – horse: *A horse can run fast, but I can run faster.*

b) sing – beautiful – bird

c) swim – good – duck (*Ente*)

d) act (*sich verhalten*) – clever – fox

e) move – quiet – mouse

f) fight – aggressive (*aggressiv*) – bull (*Stier*)

g) eat – slow – cow

h) dance – elegant – snake (*Schlange*)

i) bark – angry – dog

j) work – hard – bee (*Biene*)

## Aufgabe 6: More about your talents

**Bilde mindestens fünf Sätze, die wie der Beispielsatz aufgebaut sind, und schreibe sie auf. Benutze dazu noch einmal die unter Aufgabe 5 vorgegebenen Satzbausteine sowie deine eigenen Ideen.**

Beispiel: a) *I can run faster than a horse, but I can't run as fast as a racing car.*

## Aufgabe 7: Comparing football players

**Vielleicht bist du genau wie Tim ein großer Fußballfan? Vergleiche die Fähigkeiten und Verhaltensweisen von drei Fußballspielern mithilfe von Adverbien und deren Steigerungsformen.**

Beispiel: a) *David runs quickly, Stefan runs more quickly and Paolo runs most quickly.*

| | David | Stefan | Paolo |
|---|---|---|---|
| a) run – quick | * | ** | *** |
| b) move – elegant | ** | * | *** |
| c) play – fair | *** | ** | * |
| d) kick – hard | * | *** | ** |
| e) perform tricks – good | *** | * | ** |
| f) eat – healthy | ** | *** | * |
| g) act – bad | *** | ** | * |
| h) celebrate a goal (*ein Tor feiern*) – happy | ** | * | *** |
| i) talk – interesting | * | *** | ** |
| j) smile – nice | ** | * | *** |

## Aufgabe 8: More comparisons

**Benutze noch einmal die Tabelle aus Aufgabe 7, um Vergleiche im Satz mit Adverbien zu bilden. Bilde Satzpaare nach dem im Beispiel vorgegebenen Muster und schreibe sie auf.**

Beispiel: a) *Stefan doesn't run as quickly as Paolo, but he runs more quickly than David.*

# Abschlusstest online 9

Toll! Du hast das **Kapitel 9 – Adverbien** durchgearbeitet. In diesem Kapitel hast du dir noch einmal klar gemacht, dass es ein Unterschied ist, ob man ein Ding oder eine Person näher beschreibt (mit Adjektiven), oder ob man beschreibt, auf welche Art und Weise etwas passiert (mit Adverbien). Im Deutschen hört man diesen Unterschied nicht; im Englischen schon. Außerdem ging es darum, wie man mit Adverbien Vergleiche anstellt.

**So funktioniert der Abschlusstest online:**
Um deinen Lernerfolg zu überprüfen, kannst du nun die Abschlusstests machen. Gehe auf
**https://www.klett-lerntraining.de/9Y2A**
und wähle das Kapitel und einen Test aus.

Welche Tests es gibt, siehst du unten in der Tabelle. Nach jedem Test bekommst du eine Auswertung.

Willst du immer im Blick haben, welche Themen du schon kannst oder was du besser wiederholen solltest? Dann schreibe deine Ergebnisse in die Tabelle.

## Mein Ergebnis im Abschlusstest online – Kapitel 9

| Thema | Mein Ergebnis |
|---|---|
| Bildung und Gebrauch von Adverbien | |
| Die Steigerung von Adverbien | |

# 10 Fragen

## 10.1 Entscheidungsfragen und Kurzantworten

**Entscheidungsfragen** sind Fragen, auf die du nur mit Ja oder Nein antworten kannst. Du bildest sie , indem du das **Hilfsverb** an den **Satzanfang** ziehst.

| | | |
|---|---|---|
| You | **are** | hungry. |
| **Are** | you | hungry? |

Wenn im *simple present* und im *simple past* nur ein Vollverb im Satz steht, verwendest du ***to do*** als Hilfsverb, um die Frage zu bilden (siehe Beispiele in den Tabellen unter *simple present* und *simple past*).

Entgegnen kannst du auf Entscheidungsfragen mit einer **Kurzantwort**. Hierzu verwendest du erneut das Hilfsverb der Frage.

Bei der **bejahten Kurzantwort** verwendest du die **Langformen** der Hilfsverben, bei den **verneinten Kurzantworten** die **Kurzformen**.

### Entscheidungsfragen im *simple present*

| **Hilfsverb** | **Frage** | **Bejahte Kurzantwort** | **Verneinte Kurzantwort** |
|---|---|---|---|
| **to be** | **Are you** ready?<br>**Is he** ready? | Yes, **I am**.<br>Yes, **he is**. | No, **I'm not**.<br>No, **he isn't**. |
| **to have got** | **Have you** got a key?<br>**Has he** got …? | Yes, **I have**.<br>Yes, **he has**. | No, **I haven't**.<br>No, **he hasn't**. |
| **to do** | **Do you** smoke?<br>**Does he** smoke? | Yes, **I do**.<br>Yes, **he does**. | No, **I don't**.<br>No, **he doesn't**. |
| **Modalverb** | **Can you** swim?<br>**Can he** swim? | Yes, **I can**.<br>Yes, **he can**. | No, **I can't**.<br>No, **he can't**. |

### Entscheidungsfragen im *present progressive*

| Hilfsverb | Frage | Bejahte Kurzantwort | Verneinte Kurzantwort |
|---|---|---|---|
| **to be** | **Are you** reading?<br>**Is he** smiling? | Yes, **I am.**<br>Yes, **he is.** | No, **I'm not.**<br>No, **he isn't.** |

### Entscheidungsfragen im *simple past*

| | | | |
|---|---|---|---|
| **to be** | **Were you** there?<br>**Was he** there? | Yes, **I was.**<br>Yes, **he was.** | No, **I wasn't.**<br>No, **he wasn't.** |
| **to do** | **Did you** walk?<br>**Did he** walk? | Yes, **I did.**<br>Yes, **he did.** | No, **I didn't.**<br>No, **he didn't.** |

### Entscheidungsfragen im *past progressive*

| | | | |
|---|---|---|---|
| **to be** | **Were you** singing?<br>**Was he** singing? | Yes, **I was.**<br>Yes, **he was.** | No, **I wasn't.**<br>No, **he wasn't.** |

### Entscheidungsfragen im *present perfect*

| | | | |
|---|---|---|---|
| **to have** | **Have you** seen …?<br>**Has he** seen …? | Yes, **I have.**<br>Yes, **he has.** | No, **I haven't.**<br>No, **he hasn't.** |

### Entscheidungsfragen im *going to-future*

| | | | |
|---|---|---|---|
| **to be** | **Are you** going to help?<br>**Is he** going to help? | Yes, **I am.**<br>Yes, **he is.** | No, **I'm not.**<br>No, **he isn't.** |

### Entscheidungsfragen im *will-future*

| | | | |
|---|---|---|---|
| **will** | **Will you** come?<br>**Will he** come? | Yes, **I will.**<br>Yes, **he will.** | No, **I won't.**<br>No, **he won't.** |

## Aufgabe 1: Are you an adventurer?

**Dieser Test zeigt dir, ob du ein(e) Abenteurer(in) bist. Formuliere Entscheidungsfragen im *simple present* und antworte wahrheitsgemäß mit Ja oder Nein (Kurzantwort). Die Auflösung des Tests findest du im Lösungsteil.**

a) touch snakes and spiders (*Schlangen und Spinnen*)

Do you touch snakes and spiders?

b) swim in ice-cold water

c) go outside during a thunderstorm

d) walk into a dark forest (*Wald*) at night

e) climb steep (*steil*) rocks

f) dream of a bungee-jump

g) like roller-coaster rides (*Achterbahnfahrten*)

h) eat flies and worms (*Fliegen und Würmer*)

## Aufgabe 2: Right or wrong?

**Suzy und Tim hören im Unterricht heute viele richtige, aber auch falsche Aussagen von ihren Mitschülern. Forme diese Aussagen in Entscheidungsfragen im *simple present* um und entscheide dann, ob du mit Ja oder Nein antworten musst (Kurzantwort).**

a) Berlin is the capital of the USA.

Is Berlin the capital of the USA? No, it isn't.

b) Mice are the biggest animals on earth.

c) You can visit many sights in New York.

d) Germany has got a king.

e) Polar bears (*Eisbären*) live in Africa.

f) The River Thames runs through London.

g) The English have got many kinds (*Sorten*) of tea.

h) Penguins (*Pinguine*) can fly.

## Aufgabe 3: Suzy's morning at school

**Bilde Entscheidungsfragen und Kurzantworten im *present progressive* zu den Aktivitäten der Schüler in Suzys Klasse.**

a) Luke – write a test?

b) Megan – ask a question?

c) Josh + Harry – listen to the teacher?

d) Sophie – do maths?

## Aufgabe 4: April's fool

**Bilde mithilfe der im Text verwendeten Verben Entscheidungsfragen im *simple past*. Beantworte diese Fragen jeweils mit der zutreffenden Kurzantwort und schreibe sie auf.**

Because it was the 1st of April, Suzy and Tim played a trick on their father. When he came out of the shower in the morning, Suzy shouted: "Oh Dad, what has happened to your hair? Has it turned green?" At first, Mr Singasong just laughed. But Tim also looked shocked when he saw his father and said: "Dad, you can't go to work like that. Have you become a punk?" So Mr Singasong hurried back into the bathroom to look into the mirror and Suzy and Tim quickly ran away …

a) ______________ Suzy and Tim ______________ a trick on their father on the 1st of April?

b) ______________ Mr Singasong ______________ about Suzy's question?

c) ______________ Tim ______________ shocked when he saw his father?

d) ______________ Mr Singasong ______________ back into the bathroom to look into the mirror?

e) ______________ Suzy and Tim ______________ away after their trick?

f) ______________ Mr Singasong ______________ to work as a punk?

## Aufgabe 5: A soccer match on TV

**Familie Singasong tat alles Mögliche nebenbei, während das Fußballspiel Deutschland – England im Fernsehen lief. Bilde Entscheidungsfragen und Kurzantworten im *past progressive*.**

a) Tim – eat crisps? ✓

Was Tim eating crisps? – Yes, he was.

b) Suzy – drink coke? ✓

c) Mr Singasong – read the newspaper? ✗

d) Mrs Singasong – do a crossword puzzle? ✓

e) Lily – sit on the sofa? ✓

f) Tim and Suzy – have a fight? ✗

g) Mrs Singasong – phone her mother? ✗

h) Mr Singasong – blow his horn (*hupen*)? ✗

## Aufgabe 6: Are you a true best friend?

**In diesem Test geht es um das Thema Freundschaft. Formuliere Entscheidungsfragen im *present perfect* und antworte wahrheitsgemäß mit Ja oder Nein (Kurzantwort). Die Auflösung des Tests findest du im Lösungsteil.**

a) buy the wrong present for your best friend's birthday

Have you ever bought the wrong present for your best friend's birthday?

b) tell a lie to your best friend

c) steal anything from your best friend

d) talk badly about your best friend

e) be jealous (*eifersüchtig*) of your best friend

f) hide a secret from your best friend

g) kiss your best friend's boyfriend/girlfriend

h) forget to call your best friend

## Aufgabe 7: Lily's plans for the day

**Lily, die Katze der Familie Singasong, hat heute noch einiges vor. Bilde zu den Aktivitäten Entscheidungsfragen und Kurzantworten im *going to-future*.**

a) drink some milk – not eat a mouse

Is Lily going to go drink some milk? Yes, she is.
Is she going to eat a mouse? No, she isn't.

b) get some sleep – not go for a walk

c) play with her ball – not stay in her basket

d) fight with Tim – not sleep again

## Aufgabe 8: The world in the year 2050

**Wie stellst du dir die Welt im Jahr 2050 vor? Ergänze die Entscheidungsfragen mit den unten stehenden Verben im *will-future*. Entscheide dich dann für eine passende Kurzantwort und schreibe sie auf.**

**speak – buy – fly – be – spend – see – serve**

a) ______________ all people ______________ Chinese?

b) ______________ robots ______________ breakfast?

c) ______________ tourists ______________ their holidays on Mars?

d) ______________ all houses ______________ skyscrapers?

e) ______________ cars ______________ from one place to another?

f) ______________ we ______________ palm-trees (*Palmen*) at the North Pole (*Nordpol*)?

g) ______________ we ______________ everything in online shops?

## 10.2 Fragen nach Objekt/adverbialer Bestimmung

### Fragewörter

**Fragewörter** stehen immer am **Anfang der Frage** vor dem Hilfsverb.

| | | |
|---|---|---|
| **Who ...?** | Wem ...?/Wen ...? | fragt nach Personen |
| **What ...?** | Was ...? | fragt nach Sachen |
| **Where ...?** | Wo ...?/Woher ...?/ Wohin ...? | fragt nach einem Ort/ einer Richtung |
| **When ...?** | Wann ...? | fragt nach einem Zeitpunkt |
| **Why ...?** | Warum ...? | fragt nach dem Grund |
| **How ...?** | Wie ...? | fragt nach der Art und Weise |

- Mit ***who*** und ***what*** kannst du nach einem Objekt fragen.
- Mit ***where***, ***when***, ***why*** und ***how*** kannst du nach einer adverbialen Bestimmung fragen (sie gibt die näheren Umstände einer Handlung an).

Auch bei den Fragen mit Fragewörtern brauchst du im *simple present* und im *simple past* die **Umschreibung mit *to do***, wenn kein Hilfsverb im Satz vorhanden ist.

### Fragen im *simple present*

| Hilfsverb | Frage | | | | |
|---|---|---|---|---|---|
| **to be** | **How old** | **are** | you? | | |
| | **Where** | **is** | my bag? | | |
| **to have got** | **What** | **have** | you | got? | |
| | **Where** | **has** | he | got | it? |
| **to do** | **When** | **do** | you | meet? | |
| | **Why** | **does** | she | cry? | |
| **Modalverb** | **Where** | **can** | you | buy | it? |
| | **When** | **can** | he | see | you? |

**Fragen im *present progressive***

| Hilfsverb | Frage | | | | |
|---|---|---|---|---|---|
| **to be** | **Where**<br>**Why** | **are**<br>**is** | you<br>he | going?<br>laughing? | |

**Fragen im *simple past***

| | | | | | |
|---|---|---|---|---|---|
| **to be** | **Where**<br>**How** | **were**<br>**was** | you?<br>he? | | |
| **to do** | **What**<br>**When** | **did**<br>**did** | you<br>he | see<br>come? | there? |

**Fragen im *past progressive***

| | | | | | |
|---|---|---|---|---|---|
| **to be** | **Why**<br>**Where** | **were**<br>**was** | you<br>he | sleeping?<br>going? | |

**Fragen im *present perfect***

| | | | | | |
|---|---|---|---|---|---|
| **have** | **Where**<br>**What** | **have**<br>**has** | you<br>he | found<br>written | this?<br>so far? |

**Fragen im *will-future***

| | | | | | |
|---|---|---|---|---|---|
| **will** | **How**<br>**Where** | **will**<br>**will** | you<br>he | get<br>fly? | there? |

**Fragen im *going to-future***

| | | | | | |
|---|---|---|---|---|---|
| **to be** | **Where**<br>**What** | **is**<br>**are** | she<br>you | going to<br>going to | go?<br>do? |

## Aufgabe 9: Tourists' questions

**Suzy und Tim leben in London. Sie werden häufig von Touristen um Rat gefragt. Schreibe die Fragen in der richtigen Reihenfolge auf.**

a) to London Zoo – how – I – do – get

b) to the next bus station – the way – what – is

c) buy – can – I – a bottle of water – where

d) I – what – do – can – at the British Museum

e) must – for a tube ticket – I – pay – how much

f) the next guided tour – at the Tower – when – is

g) Bobbies – why – British policemen – are – called

h) at Buckingham Palace – see – I – who – can

i) the London Dungeon – when – close – does

j) where – Sherlock Holmes's house – I – find – can

## Aufgabe 10: Watching people in London

**In London gibt es eine Menge Leute zu beobachten. Frage nach dem unterstrichenen Satzteil.**

a) This woman is reading a book <u>on the tube</u>.

b) That woman is drinking <u>a cup of tea</u>.

c) This man is buying <u>a chicken sandwich</u>.

d) That man is laughing <u>because of a joke</u>.

e) These girls are going <u>to the London Eye</u>.

f) Those girl are lying <u>in the grass in Hyde Park</u>.

g) These boys are going to the concert <u>by bus</u>.

h) Those boys are wearing <u>their school uniforms</u>.

i) These people are waiting <u>in front of Buckingham Palace</u>.

j) Those people are watching <u>the street artists</u> (*Straßenkünstler*).

## Aufgabe 11: An interview with Freddy Fantastic

**Freddy Fantastic, der berühmte Schauspieler, gibt ein Interview. Der Moderator hat sich vorher Notizen zu den Fragen macht, die er stellen möchte. Bilde aus den Stichpunkten vollständige Fragen im *simple past* und schreibe sie auf.**

a) how – become an actor

b) when – start acting

c) what – do to get famous

d) where – play your first role

e) how – learn about your talent

f) why – be in Hollywood last month

g) when – hear about your Academy Award (*Oscar*)

h) how – your mother react to your prize

i) what – your wife say about your prize

j) where – go after the Academy Awards party

## Aufgabe 12: More questions for Freddy Fantastic

**Schreibe die folgenden Fragen an Freddy Fantastic, bei denen es um die Oscar-Party geht, in der richtigen Reihenfolge auf.**

a) wearing – what – your wife – was – at the party

b) who – sitting – at your table – was – with you

c) for dinner – were – you – having – what

d) laughing – you – why – so much – were

e) what – talking about – were – you – during the dinner

f) telling – were – you – your film partners – what

g) why – your wife – looking – was – so angry

h) your five big dogs – where – during the party – were

## Aufgabe 13: Friday 13th

**Heute sind bei Familie Singasong schon viele Missgeschicke passiert. Ob es daran liegt, dass Freitag, der 13., ist? Frage nach den unterstrichenen Satzteilen.**

a) Mr Singasong has broken a cup in the kitchen.

b) Tim has slipped (*ausgerutscht*) because of the icy street.

c) Mrs Singasong has lost an earring in the bathroom.

d) Suzy has left her exercise book at home.

e) Mr and Mrs Singasong haven't remembered to call Suzy's teacher.

f) Mrs Singasong has thrown an important letter into the dustbin (*Mülleimer*).

g) Mr Singasong has put on two different socks.

h) Tim has left his house keys on his desk.

i) Mrs Singasong's car hasn't started because of the cold.

j) Suzy has used salt instead of sugar for her tea.

## Aufgabe 14: Talking about your plans

**Bilde aus den vorgegebenen Stichworten Fragen im *going to-future* und schreibe sie auf.**

a) What – do in your holidays:

What are you going to do in your holidays?

b) When – go to bed tonight

c) Where – spend your weekend

d) Why – use the internet

e) Who – meet at school

f) When – do your homework

g) What – tell your friend

h) When – practise your English again

## Aufgabe 15: Questions about your future

**Wie sieht wohl deine Zukunft aus? Setze das angegebene Verb im *will-future* in die Lücken ein und ergänze außerdem passende Fragewörter.**

a) ____________ ____________ my future ____________ like? (be)

b) ____________ ____________ I ____________? (live)

c) ____________ ____________ I ____________ school? (finish)

d) ____________ ____________ I ____________ children? (have)

e) ____________ ____________ I ____________? (work)

f) ____________ ____________ I ____________ as a job? (do)

g) ____________ ____________ I ____________ a partner? (find)

## Aufgabe 16: The Singasongs are angry

**Manchmal ärgert sich bei den Singasongs jeder über jeden. Frage jeweils nach dem unterstrichenen Satzteil. Achtung: Es werden verschiedene Zeiten verwendet!**

a) Tim always uses <u>Suzy's hair brush</u> (*Bürste*).

b) Now Suzy is hiding Tim's hair gel <u>in her cupboard</u>.

c) So Tim is going to put <u>a plastic spider</u> in his sister's bed.

d) <u>Yesterday</u> Mrs Singasong took Suzy's mobile phone without asking her.

e) <u>Because of this</u> Suzy was using her mother's phone for a three hours' call.

f) But Suzy must pay <u>the bill (*Rechnung*) for this phone call</u> with her pocket money.

g) Mr Singasong <u>has eaten his wife's favourite chocolate bar</u>.

h) Mrs Singasong is drinking <u>all of her husband's favourite fruit juice</u> now.

i) In the end everybody will feel <u>very angry</u>.

## 10.3 Fragen nach dem Subjekt

Die Fragewörter *who* und *what* können nicht nur **Objekt** des Fragesatzes sein (siehe Kapitel 10.2), sondern auch **Subjekt**. In diesem Fall ist die Satzstellung der Frage identisch mit der Satzstellung des Aussagesatzes. Im *simple present* und *simple past* brauchst du **nicht** die Umschreibung mit dem Hilfsverb ***to do*** – es sei denn, die Frage ist verneint.

| Aussagesatz | Fragesatz |
|---|---|
| Tim talks in every lesson. | **Who** talks in every lesson? |
| This drives his teacher crazy. | **What** drives his teacher crazy? |
| Tim doesn't listen to the teacher. | **Who** doesn't listen to the teacher? |

### Aufgabe 17: A strange cat

**Eines Morgens findet Familie Singasong in ihrer Küche einen fremden Kater an der Milchschüssel der Katze Lily. Die Singasongs verteilen daher Zettel an ihre Nachbarn, um etwas darüber herauszufinden, wo der Kater herkommt. Setze *who* oder *what* ein.**

a) ____________ has seen this cat?

b) ____________ knows anything about its owner?

c) ____________ feeds the cat normally?

d) ____________ is the name of the cat?

e) ____________ makes the cat angry?

f) ____________ opened our kitchen window last night?

g) ____________ happened in our kitchen at night?

## Aufgabe 18: More information about the cat

**Frage mit *who* oder *what* nach dem unterstrichenen Wort beziehungsweise Satzteil. Achtung: In einigen Sätzen musst du nach dem Objekt, in anderen nach dem Subjekt fragen!**

a) Lily was in the Singasongs' kitchen at night.

b) She heard a strange noise in the garden.

c) Then she saw Carl the cat at the kitchen window.

d) The window was open.

e) Carl climbed through the window into the kitchen.

f) He wanted food.

g) Carl drank Lily's milk.

h) Lily didn't feel happy about that.

## Aufgabe 19: A private detective's help

**Da niemand etwas über die fremde Katze weiß, hat Familie Singsasong einen Privatdetektiv engagiert. Stelle seine Fragen, indem du nach den unterstrichenen Satzteilen fragst. Verwende dazu *who*, *what*, *where*, *when*, *why* oder *how*.**

a) We have called you because we need your help.

b) Our problem is a strange cat.

c) The cat came to our house last weekend.

d) Suzy and Tim found the cat.

e) It was in the kitchen.

f) The strange cat was just drinking Lily's milk.

g) The cat has acted wildly since then.

h) It has broken all those milk bottles over there.

i) It has destroyed (*zerstört*) some important letters.

j) Only food makes the cat calm.

k) We don't want to keep the cat because of all that chaos.

## 10.4 Bestätigungsfragen (*question tags*)

Bestätigungsfragen (*question tags*) verwendest du, wenn du von deinem Gesprächspartner Zustimmung zu einer Aussage erwartest. Die Bestätigungsfrage hängst du an den Aussagesatz an.

Du bildest die Bestätigungsfrage mit dem Hilfsverb des Aussagesatzes. Ist nur ein Vollverb im Aussagesatz vorhanden, verwendest du eine Form des Hilfsverbs *to do* zur Bildung der Frage.

Ist der Aussagesatz bejaht, wird die Bestätigungsfrage verneint:

| **Bejahter Aussagesatz** | **Verneinte Bestätigungsfrage** |
|---|---|
| This **is** your bag, | **isn't it?** |
| He **has** got two brothers, | **hasn't he?** |
| She **can** swim well, | **can't she?** |
| This cake **smells** nice, | **doesn't it?** |
| It **was** a big surprise, | **wasn't it?** |
| They **wrote** a mail yesterday, | **didn't they?** |

Ist der Aussagesatz verneint, wird die Bestätigungsfrage bejaht:

| **Verneinter Aussagesatz** | **Bejahte Bestätigungsfrage** |
|---|---|
| This **isn't** your coat, | **is it?** |
| He **hasn't** got any sisters, | **has he?** |
| She **can't** draw well, | **can she?** |
| This cake **doesn't look** bad, | **does it?** |
| It **wasn't** a terrible film, | **was it?** |
| They **didn't send** you a letter, | **did they?** |

**Beachte:**
Das Subjekt des Aussagesatzes wird in der Bestätigungsfrage zum Pronomen.

## Aufgabe 20: Tim's new girlfriend

**Vor einiger Zeit hat Tim ein Mädchen namens Ella kennengelernt. Suzy möchte alles darüber wissen. Ergänze Suzys Vermutungen passend mit den angegebenen Bestätigungsfragen.**

**am I – does she – doesn't she – has she – hasn't she – is she – isn't she – can she – can't she – do you – don't you – will you – won't you – didn't you**

a) You met at Ella at school, ________________?

b) She is new in your tutor group, ________________?

c) She has got a nice name, ________________?

d) You really like her, ________________?

e) You will bring her to our house, ________________?

f) She comes from Edinburgh, ________________?

g) She can speak Scottish, ________________?

h) But she can't play the bagpipe (*Dudelsack*), ________________?

i) And she hasn't got a kilt (*Schottenrock*), ________________?

j) She doesn't know many people here, ________________?

k) She isn't in love with you, ________________?

l) You won't see her tonight, ________________?

m) I am not getting on your nerves, ________________?

## Aufgabe 21: Ella is talking to Suzy

**Ella spricht Suzy auf dem Pausenhof an, denn auch sie ist neugierig und möchte viel über Tim wissen. Bilde passende Bestätigungsfragen zu Ellas Aussagen.**

a) Hi, you are Tim's sister, ________________?

b) Tim hasn't got a girlfriend, ________________?

c) He is a good musician (*Musiker*), ________________?

d) He will play at this year's school concert, ________________?

e) Tim has written a song about me, ________________?

f) He didn't try to phone me yesterday, ________________?

g) He doesn't own a mobile, ________________?

h) You won't tell him about our conversation (*Gespräch*),

________________?

## Aufgabe 22: Tim's questions at school

**Tim kann sich in der Schule zur Zeit nur schlecht konzentrieren. Daher muss er oft nachfragen, worum es gerade geht oder was zu tun ist. In dieser Aufgabe sind die Bestätigungsfragen vorgegeben. Du musst die passenden Aussagesätze bilden.**

a) (not get - any homework), did we?

b) (write an English test - next week), won't we?

c) (go to assembly - every Monday morning), don't we?

d) (school band - not meet yet), has it?

# Abschlusstest online 10

Wow, gute Leistung! Du hast das **Kapitel 10 – Fragen** durchgearbeitet. Jetzt kannst du auf Englisch anderen Leuten Löcher in den Bauch fragen, egal, ob sie einfach mit Ja oder Nein antworten sollen (Entscheidungsfragen), ob du nähere Informationen von ihnen haben möchtest (Fragen mit Fragewörtern), oder ob du nur etwas bestätigt haben willst (*question tags*).

**So funktioniert der Abschlusstest online:**
Um deinen Lernerfolg zu überprüfen, kannst du nun die Abschlusstests machen. Gehe auf
**https://www.klett-lerntraining.de/9Y2A**
und wähle das Kapitel und einen Test aus.

Welche Tests es gibt, siehst du unten in der Tabelle. Nach jedem Test bekommst du eine Auswertung.

Willst du immer im Blick haben, welche Themen du schon kannst oder was du besser wiederholen solltest? Dann schreibe deine Ergebnisse in die Tabelle.

## Mein Ergebnis im Abschlusstest online – Kapitel 10

| Thema | Mein Ergebnis |
|---|---|
| Entscheidungsfragen und Kurzantworten | |
| Fragen nach Subjekt, Objekt/adverbialer Bestimmung | |
| Bestätigungsfragen (*question tags*) | |

# 11 Satzstruktur und Wortstellung

## 11.1 Stellung von Zeit- und Ortsangaben

### Aussagesätze mit Zeitangaben

Zeitangaben stehen entweder am Satzanfang oder am Satzende, d.h. vor dem Subjekt oder nach dem Objekt. Am Satzanfang ist die Zeitangabe stärker betont als am Satzende.

| Zeitangabe | Subjekt | Prädikat | Objekt | Zeitangabe |
|---|---|---|---|---|
| **Every day** | I | meet | my friends. | |
| | I | meet | my friends | **every day**. |

### Aussagesätze mit Ortsangaben

Ortsangaben stehen nach dem Objekt des Satzes.

| Subjekt | Prädikat | Objekt | Ortsangabe |
|---|---|---|---|
| I | meet | my friends | **at school**. |

### Aussagesätze mit Zeit- und Ortsangaben

| Zeitangabe | Subjekt | Prädikat | Objekt | Ortsangabe |
|---|---|---|---|---|
| **Every day** | I | meet | my friends | **at school**. |

Stehen Zeit- und Ortsangabe am Ende des Satzes, so gilt: Ort vor Zeit.

| Subjekt | Prädikat | Objekt | Ortsangabe | Zeitangabe |
|---|---|---|---|---|
| I | meet | my friends | **at school** | **every day**. |

## Aufgabe 1: Every morning

**Für die Reihenfolge der Satzglieder gibt es jeweils zwei Möglichkeiten. Schreibe beide auf.**

a) rings – my alarm clock– at 6.30 am

b) I – ten minutes later – get up

c) feel – I – especially tired – every Monday

d) but every Sunday morning – very happy – I – feel

e) every weekend – stay – in bed as long as I like – I

## Aufgabe 2: Different rooms

**Schreibe die Sätze in der richtigen Reihenfolge auf.**

a) watch – TV – I – in the living-room

b) my teeth – brush – in the bathroom – I

c) read – in my bedroom – I – books

d) have – in the kitchen – I – breakfast

e) my clothes – put – in the hall – I

## Aufgabe 3: Too many hobbies

**Schreibe auch hier wieder beide Möglichkeiten für die Reihenfolge der Satzglieder auf.**

a) practise – I – at school – the piano – every day

b) twice a week – play – I – tennis – at my tennis club

c) dancing lessons – take – I – every Wednesday – in town

d) at the gym (*Fitnesscenter*) – taekwondo – do – I – every Friday

e) on Sundays – football – play – I – on the sports ground (*Sportplatz*)

## 11.2 Stellung von Adverbien der Häufigkeit und Art und Weise

### Aussagesätze mit Adverbien der Häufigkeit

Adverbien der Häufigkeit (*adverbs of frequency*) wie *sometimes*, *often* oder *always* stehen meist direkt vor dem Vollverb. Gibt es ein Hilfsverb, so stehen sie zwischen Hilfsverb und Vollverb.

| Subjekt | Hilfs-verb | Adverb der Häufigkeit | Vollverb | |
|---|---|---|---|---|
| James | | **sometimes** | walks | to school. |
| He | can | **often** | take | his brother's bike. |

**Ausnahmen**:

- Steht im *simple present* oder *simple past* eine Form von *to be*, d.h. *am/is/are oder was/were*, als einziges Verb, dann kommt das Adverb der Häufigkeit dahinter.

  James is **always** late.

- *Sometimes* kann zur besonderen Betonung am Satzanfang stehen.

  **Sometimes** he isn't late.

### Aussagesätze mit Adverbien der Art und Weise

Adverbien der Art und Weise (*adverbs of manner*, siehe auch Kapitel 9.1) stehen direkt nach dem Vollverb, wenn es kein Objekt gibt:

| Subjekt | Verb | Adverb | |
|---|---|---|---|
| James | sings | **terribly** | in the car every day. |

Sonst stehen Adverbien der Art und Weise in der Regel direkt nach dem direkten Objekt.

| Subjekt | Verb | Objekt | Adverb | |
|---|---|---|---|---|
| James | sings | most songs | **terribly** | in the car every day. |

## Aufgabe 4: Sometimes or never?

**Schreibe die Sätze in der richtigen Reihenfolge auf. Falls es zwei Möglichkeiten gibt, notiere beide.**

a) a lot of chocolate – can – sometimes – Tim – eat

b) never – he – sick – feels – after that

c) Suzy – watches – action films – never – alone

d) sometimes – but – them – must – she – watch – with Tim

e) trouble – sometimes – have – Suzy and Tim – with each other

f) never – but – they – tell – about it – their parents

## Aufgabe 5: Always

**Schreibe die Sätze auf und setze dabei *always* an der richtigen Stelle ein.**

a) He is polite. But she doesn't answer in a friendly way.

b) They must do their homework. They must show it to the teacher.

c) We were happy as children. We spent a lot of time outdoors (*draußen*).

d) They have lived in this house. They have liked it here a lot.

e) You will be my best friend. I will be there for you.

## Aufgabe 6: Well or badly?

**Forme Adverbien aus den Wörtern in Klammern und setze sie an der richtigen Stelle im Satz ein.**

a) Lily can't sing. She cries at night in the Singasongs' house. (beautiful/terrible)

b) Suzy plays the saxophone. But she whistles (*pfeift*) from time to time. (fantastic/awful)

c) Suzy's mum rides her bike. But she drives her taxi every day. (bad/good)

d) Tim walks to school. But he runs home in the evening. (slow/fast)

## 11.3 *If*-Sätze im *present tense*

### Gebrauch und Bildung von Bedingungssätzen (*if-clauses*)

Mit einem *if*-Satz im *simple present* drückst du eine **erfüllbare Bedingung** aus. Im dazu gehörigen **Hauptsatz** steht, welche **Folge für die Zukunft** sich ergibt, falls diese Bedingung erfüllt wird.

Du kannst im Hauptsatz *will-future*, Modalverben oder den Imperativ (die Befehlsform) in der bejahten oder der verneinten Form verwenden.

| | ***if*-Satz** | **Hauptsatz** |
|---|---|---|
| *will-future* | **If** we **win** the match, | we **will be** very happy. |
| | **If** we **don't win** the match, | we **won't get** a prize. |
| Modalverben | **If** you **get up** early, | you **can have** breakfast with me. |
| | **If** you **don't get up** early, | you **can't catch** the bus. |
| Imperativ | **If** you **are** cold, | **close** the window. |
| | **If** you **aren't** cold, | **don't put** on more clothes. |

Der Hauptsatz kann auch vor dem *if*-Satz stehen:
He **will eat** the whole cake **if** he **gets** it.

### *If* und *when*

Das deutsche **wenn** wird im Englischen je nach Situation mit ***if*** (falls) oder ***when*** (zu dem Zeitpunkt, wenn) wiedergegeben:

**If** I **get** a mail from Lucy, I will answer it at once.
→ Es ist möglich, aber nicht sicher, dass Lucy eine Mail schreibt.

**When** I **get** a mail from Lucy, I will answer it at once.
→ Es ist sicher, dass Lucy eine Mail schreibt.

## Aufgabe 7: Winning the lottery

**Mrs Singasong träumt davon, im Lotto zu gewinnen. Bilde eine Kette mit *if*-Sätzen, die zeigt, wie Mrs Singasong sich ihr neues Leben vorstellt.**

a) win/be a millionaire: *If she wins, she will be a millionaire.*

b) stop working: *If she is a millionaire, she* ______________________.

c) have lots of free time ______________________

d) travel to other countries ______________________

e) not see her family much ______________________

f) not be happy ______________________

g) not care about all the money ______________________

## Aufgabe 8: Your ideas about winning the lottery

**Vielleich träumst ja auch du von einem Lottogewinn? Bilde erneut eine Kette mit *if*-Sätzen, diesmal in der 1. Person Singular. Setze die Kette mit mindestens drei eigenen Ideen fort.**

a) win/have lots of money: *If I win, I will have lots of money.*

b) go shopping every day: *If I have lots of money, I …* ______________________

c) not have time for my homework ______________________

d) get into trouble ______________________

## Aufgabe 9: Help yourself

**Kombiniere die Bausteine unten miteinander, sodass du jeweils einen *if*-Satz mit Imperativ-Hauptsatz erhältst. Schreibe die Sätze auf.**

Beispiel: a) *If you are cold, close the window.*

| | | |
|---|---|---|
| ~~cold~~ | drink | for a long run |
| hungry | talk | some sleep |
| nervous | do | a glass of water |
| tired | ~~close~~ | about it to a friend |
| thirsty | go | some yoga exercises |
| sad | get | yourself a sandwich |
| angry | make | ~~the window~~ |

## Aufgabe 10: Tips for tourists in London

**Formuliere hilfreiche Hinweise für Touristen in London in Form von *if*-Sätzen und Hauptsätzen mit Modalverb. Kombiniere dazu die Bausteine unten und schreibe die Sätze auf.**

Beispiel: a) *If you go to Madame Tussaud's, you can see Michael Jackson in wax.*

| | | |
|---|---|---|
| ~~go to Madame Tussaud's~~ | | try the shops on Oxford Street |
| stay for a week | should | watch a play at the Globe Theatre |
| | can | |
| be interested in theatre | must | make a picnic in Hyde Park |
| want to do some shopping | | ~~see Michael Jackson in wax~~ |
| visit Buckingham Palace | | go to Portobello Market |
| enjoy parks | | buy a one-week tube ticket |
| like old things | | take a look at the guards |

## Aufgabe 11: Tim's plans

**Tim macht sich Gedanken über seine Pläne für die nächsten Tage und Wochen. Setze *if* oder *when* in die Lücken ein.**

a) ________________ the weather is good, I will go for a ride with my bike on Sunday.

b) I will stay at home and learn for my math test ________________ the weather is bad.

c) ________________ granddad turns 70 next month, I will play a drums solo for him.

d) ________________ he doesn't like my music, I will be very sad.

e) I will be very tired again tomorrow ________________ I stay up too long tonight.

f) But ________________ the holidays start, I will sleep for a whole week.

g) ________________ Suzy gets on my nerves the next time, I will simply not listen to her.

h) I will never talk to her again ________________ she tells Mum and Dad about my feelings for Ella.

i) ________________ I see Ella at school again, I will ask her for a date.

j) ________________ she likes me, she will say yes.

## 11.4 Notwendige Relativsätze mit und ohne Relativpronomen

Notwendige Relativsätze (*defining relative clauses*) definieren das Wort, auf das sie sich beziehen, näher. Man kann sie nicht einfach weglassen, ohne den Sinn des Satzes zu verändern. Sie werden durch ein Relativpronomen eingeleitet, das Objekt oder Subjekt des Relativsatzes sein kann. Vor notwendigen Relativsätzen steht im Englischen, anders als im Deutschen, kein Komma.

### Relativpronomen als Subjekt des Relativsatzes

| | | |
|---|---|---|
| Personen im Singular und im Plural | **who**<br>**that** | Many people **who/that** live in London use the underground every day. |
| Dinge im Singular und im Plural | **which**<br>**that** | The house **which/that** is yellow is our house. |

### Relativpronomen als Objekt des Relativsatzes

| | | |
|---|---|---|
| Personen im Singular und im Plural | **whom**<br>**who**<br>**that** | The girl **whom/who/that** you can see in the picture is my sister. |
| Dinge im Singular und im Plural | **which**<br>**that** | The car **which/that** we want to buy is very big. |

***Whom*** wird in der förmlichen geschriebenen Sprache verwendet, ***who*** und ***that*** werden jedoch häufiger benutzt.

Die Relativpronomen können weggelassen werden, wenn sie Objekt des Relativsatzes sind (nur dann!). Diese Art der Relativsätze nennt man ***contact clauses***:

The girl you can see in the picture is my sister.

The car we want to buy is very big.

### Das Relativpronomen *whose*

Das Relativpronomen ***whose*** steht immer vor einem Nomen. Es drückt aus, wem etwas gehört oder zu wem etwas gehört.

| | | |
|---|---|---|
| Personen im Singular und im Plural | **whose** | The boy **whose** hair is black is my brother. |
| Dinge im Singular und im Plural | **whose** | The house **whose** door is red looks nice. |

## Aufgabe 12: Young people and the internet

**Setze *who* oder *which* in die Lücken ein.**

A lot of young people (a) ____________ grow up today often use computers (b) ____________ they sometimes have in their own rooms. The parents (c) ____________ didn't have computers in their youth (*Jugend*) often don't know a lot about the things (d) ____________ their children do on the internet. The time (e) ____________ many children (f) ____________ own a computer spend on the internet is often very long. A problem (g) ____________ is very big is that on the internet, some children give too much information to people (h) ____________ they don't know. But a thing (i) ____________ some people forget is that the information (j) ____________ you can find on the internet can also be very useful.

## Aufgabe 13: Suzy's tutor group

**Suzy spricht über ihre Mitschüler. Verbinde die Sätze mithilfe von Relativpronomen. Schreibe sie auf.**

a) The girl is called Olivia. She is sitting next to me.

*The girl who is sitting next to me is called Olivia.*

b) The jacket is hers. It has black stripes on it.

c) The boy is called George. He has got red hair.

d) The blue pen was my present. He always uses it.

e) The girl's name is Sophie. She lives in my street.

f) She has a skateboard. She rides it every day.

g) The boy is a good friend of mine. His name his Daniel.

h) The shoes look very smart. Their colour is black.

i) The girl is called Lisa. She plays football.

j) She often wears a T-shirt. She got it from a famous football player.

## Aufgabe 14: Grammar exercises

**Gib alle Relativpronomen an, die du jeweils in die Lücken einsetzen kannst. Bilde außerdem, falls möglich, *contact clauses*, und schreibe sie auf.**

a) The exercises ____________ you can find in this book are all about grammar.

b) Maybe it has helped you with some of the problems ____________ you have had with grammar.

c) The exercises ____________ are easy can be done quickly.

d) Exercises ____________ you must work on longer are more difficult.

e) The pupils ____________ have done all the exercises have done a very good job.

# Abschlusstest online 11

Großartig! Du hast das **Kapitel 11 – Satzstruktur und Wortstellung** durchgearbeitet. Dabei hast du dir noch einmal ins Gedächtnis gerufen, an welche Stelle im Satz Orts- und Zeitangaben und Adverbien gehören. Außerdem kannst du jetzt mit *if*-Sätzen ausdrücken, was passiert, falls eine bestimmte Bedingung eintritt. Und Relativsätze helfen dir dabei, noch mehr Informationen in einen Satz zu packen.

**So funktioniert der Abschlusstest online:**
Um deinen Lernerfolg zu überprüfen, kannst du nun die Abschlusstests machen. Gehe auf
**https://www.klett-lerntraining.de/9Y2A**
und wähle das Kapitel und einen Test aus.

Welche Tests es gibt, siehst du unten in der Tabelle. Nach jedem Test bekommst du eine Auswertung.

Willst du immer im Blick haben, welche Themen du schon kannst oder was du besser wiederholen solltest? Dann schreibe deine Ergebnisse in die Tabelle.

## Mein Ergebnis im Abschlusstest online – Kapitel 11

| Thema | Mein Ergebnis |
|---|---|
| Stellung von Orts- und Zeitangaben | |
| Stellung von Adverbien der Häufigkeit und Art und Weise | |
| *If*-Sätze im *present tense* | |
| Notwendige Relativsätze mit und ohne Relativpronomen | |

# Lösungen

# 1 Artikel und Nomen

### Aufgabe 1

In the picture you can see a family. There is a girl with a saxophone. This is Suzy Singasong. You can also see a woman. She is Suzy's mother. She is singing. On the left there is a boy. This is Tim, Suzy's brother. He is playing the drums. There is also a man with a guitar. He is Suzy's father. On the floor there is a cat. This is Lily.

a) a family b) a girl c) a saxophone d) a woman
e) a boy f) a man g) a guitar h) a cat

### Aufgabe 2

a) an English family
b) a young girl
c) a new saxophone
d) an interesting woman
e) a tall boy
f) a cool man
g) an old guitar
h) a small cat

### Aufgabe 3

a) She drives a bus. She is **a bus driver**.
b) He plays in films. He is **an actor**.
c) She sells clothes. She is **a shop assistant**.
d) He looks after houses. He is **a caretaker**.
e) She makes pizza. She is **a cook**.
f) He works for a newspaper. He is **a reporter**.
g) She is the boss of the shop. She is **a manager**.
h) He works at school. He is **a teacher**.

### Aufgabe 4

a) a banana b) an apple c) a sandwich
d) an egg e) an orange f) a cake

### Aufgabe 5

a) a bad banana b) a sour apple c) a tiny sandwich
d) an old egg e) a bitter orange f) a dry cake

### Aufgabe 6

| | [ðə] | [ði] |
|---|---|---|
| a) the uniform | ✗ | ☐ |
| b) the exercise books | ☐ | ✗ |
| c) the new pencils | ✗ | ☐ |
| d) the old ruler | ☐ | ✗ |
| e) the school bag | ✗ | ☐ |
| f) the tiny rubber | ✗ | ☐ |
| g) the big pencil-case | ✗ | ☐ |
| h) the important mobile | ☐ | ✗ |
| i) the tasty sandwiches | ✗ | ☐ |
| j) the expensive sports shoes | ☐ | ✗ |

### Aufgabe 7

a) Suzy needs **the** alarm clock next to **the** bed to wake up every morning.
b) Then she puts on **the** uniform of her school.
c) School uniforms are very important in England.
d) **The** uniform of Suzy's school is red.
e) Suzy likes **the** colour red.
f) But she doesn't like **the** woollen skirt of her uniform.
g) Suzy hates wool.
h) Suzy's school is in Einstein Road.
i) She usually goes there by bus.
j) She meets all her friends at school.
k) In the morning, she waits in front of **the** school for them.
l) She often talks to them about **the** boys in their tutor group.
m) Suzy spends a lot of time at school.
n) Sometimes she goes to **the** park behind **the** school.
o) Then she plays **the** saxophone there.

### Aufgabe 8

a) I have got **a** big room of my own.
b) In **the** room I can play **the** drums.
c) There are posters on **the** walls.
d) On **the** posters you can see famous drummers.
e) I have only **a** small wardrobe in my room.

f) The wardrobe isn't big enough for all my stuff.
g) So usually a lot of my clothes are on the floor.
h) I am not a very tidy person.
i) In my room there is also an old desk.
j) The desk is a present from my grandfather.
k) All the things for school are in the desk.
l) There are a lot of books on the shelf in the corner .
m) The books are about computers and sports.
n) Behind the door there is a pile of music magazines.
o) The best music magazine comes from Manchester.

**Aufgabe 9**

a) two cows
b) three cats
c) five mice
d) two horses
e) five sheep
f) three fish

**Aufgabe 10**

a) a face/faces
b) an eye/eyes
c) a nose/noses
d) an ear/ears
e) a mouth/mouths
f) a tooth/teeth
g) an arm/arms
h) a hand/hands
i) a leg/legs
j) a foot/feet

**Aufgabe 11**

a) tables
b) chairs
c) sofas
d) cupboards
e) pictures
f) beds
g) shelves
h) desks

**Aufgabe 12**

a) Suzy, Tim and their parents go to the circus today.
b) There are many other families like the Singasongs there.
c) Tim wants to see the three white tigers.
d) Suzy is waiting for the clown with the red nose.
e) Finally the show begins.
f) Mrs Singasong loves the two speaking parrots.
g) Mr Singasong likes the group of Chinese acrobats.
h) In the end, everybody in the audience is happy: boys and girls, men and women.

**Aufgabe 13**

a) Suzy's saxophone
b) Tim's drums
c) the family's house
d) the parents' room
e) Dad's guitar
f) Mum's clothes
g) Lily's milk
h) the neighbours' car
i) the friends' dog
j) the uncle's watch
k) the teacher's pen
l) the pupils' uniforms

## Aufgabe 14

a) a box of candles
b) a list of the guests
c) the children's ideas
d) a big bag of decorations
e) Dad's address book
f) the relatives' phone numbers
g) Mum's help
h) a book of funny games
i) the keys of the living room
j) the melody of the birthday song

## Aufgabe 15

| | s-Genitiv Singular | s-Genitiv Plural | Einfaches Plural-s | Kurzform von *has* | Kurzform von *is* |
|---|---|---|---|---|---|
| a) Tim: "Dad's work finishes at 5 pm." | ✗ | | | | |
| b) Suzy: "So he's got free time after that." | | | | ✗ | |
| c) Tim: "Okay, then the party starts at 6. That's a good idea." | | | | | ✗ |
| d) Suzy: "Everything's ready for the party?" | | | | | ✗ |
| e) Tim: "No, we still need to buy some things." | | | ✗ | | |
| f) Suzy: "Do you think we can take our parents' purse for the shopping?" | | ✗ | | | |
| g) Tim: "No, I think we need Mum's okay to take the money." | ✗ | | | | |

## Aufgabe 16

a) a pound/packet of butter
b) a box of eggs
c) a bag/packet/pound of flour
d) a bag/packet/pound of sugar
e) a bottle/packet of milk
f) a packet/bag/pound of carrots
g) a bar of chocolate
h) a bag/packet of hazelnuts
i) a bag/packet of coconut flakes
j) a glass of honey
k) a packet of candles
l) a tin of peaches

# 2 Pronomen und Begleiter

### Aufgabe 1

Hi, I'm Suzy Singasong. Do you like music? Then come and meet my family. We all play together in a band. It's called "The Singasong Family". My brother Tim practices the drums for hours every day. He often gets on my nerves. But my parents are really nice. They aren't very strict. I love our cat Lily. Sometimes she listens to our music, too. We have only got one problem: our neighbours. They don't like the noise we make.

### Aufgabe 2

a) **I**'m twelve.
b) **We**'re from London.
c) **They**'re cool.
d) **It**'s swimming.
e) **He**'s fifteen.
f) **She**'s a taxi driver.
g) **He**'s a teacher.
h) **They**'re nice.

### Aufgabe 3

a) Can you help **him** with the sandwiches?
b) Put **them** on the table, please.
c) Please phone **her**.
d) Bring **me** that one over there, please!
e) Can you pick **her** up there?
f) Get **it** at the baker's, please.
g) Can you help **us**?
h) Tell **me**, please.

### Aufgabe 4

a) Let us start the lesson now.
b) Tell me about your homework.
c) Could you say it again, please?
d) You can play the game with them.
e) Show me your pictures next week.
f) Ask her about the exercise.
g) Help him with the grammar, please.
h) You can talk about it with your neighbours.

### Aufgabe 5

a) **He** hears **it**.
b) **She** dreams about **them**.
c) **He** can't find **them**.
d) **She** calls **them**.
e) **He** tells **them**.
f) **She** plays a trick on **him**.
g) **They** eat **it**.
h) **She** looks for **it**.
i) **She** catches **it**.
j) **He** kisses **her**.

### Aufgabe 6

a) **his** drums b) **her** keyboards c) **his** guitar d) **her** voice
e) **its** song f) **their** shouts g) **its** sounds h) **her** purring

### Aufgabe 7

(a) her shoes (b) your sweatshirt (c) my sweatshirt
(d) its colour (e) my room (f) His books
(g) Their titles (h) our parents' new mobile phone

### Aufgabe 8

a) **You're** very late, Tim. Is **your** alarm clock out of order?
b) Well, **it's** not working because **its** batteries are empty. I'm sorry.
c) And what is **your** excuse, Phil? What is **your** reason for being late?
d) **It's** my bike, Sir. **Its** tyre is flat.
e) **You're** good at finding excuses. And what about **your** homework, boys?
f) **It's** my pen. **Its** ink has run out.
g) ..., but **it's** in my exercise book ... Maybe **it's** in my sister's bag.

### Aufgabe 9

(a) His (b) he's (c) He's (d) He's
(e) He's (f) his (g) his (h) His
(i) he's (j) he's

### Aufgabe 10

(a) There (b) they're (c) there (d) their
(e) Their (f) They're (g) their (h) they're
(i) there (j) their

### Aufgabe 11

a) ours b) his c) yours d) hers
e) mine f) theirs

### Aufgabe 12

(a) yours (b) mine (c) hers (d) his
(e) ours (f) yours (g) theirs

### Aufgabe 13

a) Sorry, is this your/~~yours~~ car, Madam? If it is ~~your~~/yours, please move it away.
b) No, this isn't my/~~mine~~ car, ~~my~~/mine is much smaller.
c) Is it your/~~yours~~ neighbours' car then? If it is ~~their~~/theirs, you must tell us their/~~theirs~~ names and addresses.
d) No, it is not our/~~ours~~ neighbours' car.
e) So maybe your/~~yours~~ daughter or your/~~yours~~ son own this car?
f) No, it is not ~~their~~/theirs, they are both too young to drive.
g) Okay, but do you know the owner of this car?
h) Yes, my mother is here for a cup of tea. The car is ~~her~~/hers.

### Aufgabe 14

| | | | |
|---|---|---|---|
| (a) you | (b) us | (c) my | (d) mine |
| (e) it | (f) it | (g) his/yours | (h) it |
| (i) yours/his | (j) it | (k) he | (l) my |
| (m) his | (n) I | (o) we | (p) your |

### Aufgabe 15

a) I would like to have a look at **that** scarf over there.
b) But maybe **this** scarf here is the right one?
c) No, **these** here aren't mine.
d) What about **those** white shoes over there?
e) But **this** cap here is mine.

### Aufgabe 16

| | | | |
|---|---|---|---|
| a) those | b) this | c) that | d) these |
| e) this | f) those | | |

### Aufgabe 17

| | |
|---|---|
| a) There is some milk in the fridge. | b) But there isn't any orange juice. |
| c) There is some cheese in the fridge. | d) But there aren't any bananas. |
| e) There aren't any spaghetti in the fridge. | f) But there are some eggs. |
| g) There is some butter in the fridge. | h) But there aren't any tomatoes. |
| i) There is some ham in the fridge. | j) But there aren't any potatoes. |
| k) There is some yoghurt in the fridge. | l) But there aren't any apples. |

### Aufgabe 18

a) Why don't you buy **some** tea for Lena?
b) Tea is fine but there isn't **any** in this shop here.
c) What about **some** crackers then?
d) Don't you have **any** other ideas?
e) Well, does this shop have **any** cups with pictures of the Royal family?
f) No, I can't see **any**.
g) Let's look for **some** funny cards then.
h) Okay, and maybe I'll find **some** nice pencils with the British flag on them.

### Aufgabe 19

Mögliche Sätze:
Would you like some water?/some potatoes?
Can I give you some salt?/some beans?
Can I please have some bread?/some sauce?
Could you please pass me some lemonade?/ketchup?

## 3 Das *present tense*

### Aufgabe 1

a) I **am** Tim. I **have** got a sister.
b) Suzy **is** funny. She **has** got a lot of humour.
c) Sometimes we **have** got problems and we **are** angry at each other.
d) Sometimes I **have** got trouble with my parents, but luckily they **have** got strong nerves.
e) School **is** okay. All of my friends **are** there, too.
f) One girl **is** really nice, she **has** got blue eyes.

### Aufgabe 2

a) I **am** a very big animal.
b) My voice **sounds** like a trumpet.
c) I **live** in Africa or in Asia.
d) The colour of my skin **is** grey.
e) You **call** my nose a "trunk".
f) I **carry** heavy things or people on my back.
g) Some of my brothers and sisters **work** in circuses.
h) Silly people **laugh** about my ears.

The name of the animal: **elephant**

### Aufgabe 3

a) I live in the house or in the garden.
b) Long walks are good for me.
c) I am your best friend.
d) I bark at the postman.
e) I find cats nasty.

The name of the animal: **dog**

### Aufgabe 4

be have got turn sing go need cut heat put add cook feel

| | | | |
|---|---|---|---|
| a) is | b) has got | c) turns | d) sings |
| e) goes | f) needs | g) cuts | h) heats |
| i) puts | j) adds | k) cooks | l) feels |

### Aufgabe 5

a) You aren't/are not silly.
b) She isn't/is not tall.
c) I'm not/I am not small
d) He isn't/is not young.
e) It isn't/is not new.
f) They aren't/are not nice.
g) We aren't/are not old.

### Aufgabe 6

a) They haven't got/have not got a house.
b) I haven't got/have not got a pencil.
c) She hasn't got/has not got a ball.
d) We haven't/have not got a car.
e) He hasn't got/has not got a game.
f) You haven't/have not got a sandwich.
g) It hasn't got/has not got a door.

### Aufgabe 7

a) Mr Singasong **doesn't/does not get up** at 6 o'clock.
b) Mrs Singasong **doesn't/does not drive** her taxi.
c) Tim and Suzy **don't/do not go** to school.
d) Mrs Singasong **doesn't/does not tell** her children to hurry up.
e) The cat Lily **doesn't/does not spend** so much time on her own.
f) The postman **doesn't/does not bring** the family any letters.
g) Tim and Suzy **don't/do not eat** at the school cafeteria.

### Aufgabe 8

a) He **doesn't/does not talk** to his parents.
b) He **doesn't/does not open** the door of his room.
c) He **doesn't/does not have** dinner with his family.
d) He **doesn't/does not turn off** the music in his room.

e) He **doesn't/does not answer** the phone.
f) He **doesn't/does not come** into the living room.
g) He **doesn't/does not do** his homework.

### Aufgabe 9

a) isn't/is not
b) doesn't/does not play
c) don't/do not collect
d) hasn't/has not got
e) doesn't/does not go
f) haven't/have not got
g) doesn't/does not draw
h) doesn't/does not like
i) don't/do not watch
j) aren't/are not

### Aufgabe 10

a) walking
b) running
c) riding a bike
d) swimming
e) flying
f) driving a car
g) taking a bus

### Aufgabe 11

a) They **are sitting** around a fire.
b) Tim **is playing** the guitar.
c) They **are roasting** marshmallows in the fire.
d) Suzy **is laughing** about a joke.
e) Tim's friend Nat **is eating** some bread.
f) Nat and Suzy **are talking** about their plans.
g) Suzy **is looking** into the flames.
h) All of them **are having** a good time.

### Aufgabe 12

a) The Singasongs **are spending** a weekend at the seaside in Brighton.
b) They **are having** a lot of fun on the beach.
c) Tim **is chasing** Suzy in the water.
d) Mrs Singasong **is buying** some ice-cream.
e) Mr Singasong **is reading** a book.
f) A lot of other people **are enjoying** their time on the beach, too.
g) A little child **is building** a sand castle.
h) An old man **is trying** to catch a fish.
i) A girl **is drinking** a bottle of water.
j) Another girl **is drawing** a picture of the sea.
k) A woman **is sleeping** on her sunbed.
l) A boy **is looking** at a sailing boat.
m) His brother **is calling** his girl-friend.
n) Some teenagers **are playing** volleyball.
o) A dog **is swimming** in the water.

### Aufgabe 13

a) Tim is smiling. He isn't crying.
b) Suzy is swimming. She isn't sailing.
c) The dog is sleeping. It isn't barking.
d) Tim and Suyz are running. They aren't jumping.
e) Lily and the dog are playing. They aren't fighting.
f) Lily is climbing a tree. She isn't falling down.
g) Tim is eating. He isn't cooking.
h) Suzy is watching TV. She isn't doing sports.
i) Tim and Suzy are leaving the house. They aren't arriving.

### Aufgabe 14

| | | | |
|---|---|---|---|
| a) likes | b) is drinking | c) is | d) wants |
| e) cannot/can't | f) is | g) is trying | h) cannot/can't |
| i) must | j) has | k) is not/isn't | l) climbs |
| m) is not/isn't | n) does not/doesn't know | | o) is waiting |

### Aufgabe 15

a) Usually the Singasongs **spend** their holidays at the sea, but this time they **are staying** in the Lake District.
b) Every August they **relax** on the beach, but this August they **are taking** long walks in the mountains.
c) They often **rise** late in their holidays, but today they **are getting up** at seven.
d) This year they **are staying** at a friend's house, but usually they **go** to a hotel.
e) Normally they **eat** their dinner at a restaurant in their holidays, but this time Mr Singasong **is doing** the cooking.
f) This year they **are buying** a lot of souvenirs, but usually they **don't do** a lot of shopping in their holidays.
g) Normally they **don't take** the bus in their holidays, but today they **are going** to Windermere, a small village, by bus.

# 4 Das *past tense*

### Aufgabe 1

a) explained b) corrected c) copied d) counted
e) played f) repeated g) practised

### Aufgabe 2

### Aufgabe 3

go be ride want be like watch eat feel enjoy drive cost do have

a) went b) were c) rode d) wanted
e) was f) liked g) watched h) ate
i) felt j) enjoyed k) drove l) cost
m) did n) had

### Aufgabe 4

a) The waiters weren't/were not friendly.
b) The hotel room wasn't/was not clean.
c) The swimming pool wasn't/was not warm enough.
d) The weather wasn't/was not good.
e) The prices weren't/were not cheap.
f) The hotel wasn't/was not close to the sea.
g) The shops weren't/were not interesting.

### Aufgabe 5

a) Last week the English teacher didn't/did not feel very well.
b) So she didn't/did not remember everything that was important.
c) She didn't/did not put her English book into her bag.
d) She didn't/did not take her school keys with her.
e) She didn't/did not find her watch.
f) She didn't/did not control the pupils' homework.

### Aufgabe 6

a) didn't/did not look
b) weren't/were not
c) didn't/did not use
d) didn't/did not come
e) didn't/did not know
f) wasn't/was not
g) didn't/did not scare
h) weren't/were not
i) didn't/did not enjoy
j) didn't/did not seem

### Aufgabe 7

a) didn't/did not make
b) didn't/did not chat
c) didn't/did not use
d) didn't/did not read
e) weren't/were not
f) didn't/did not take
g) didn't/did not send
h) didn't/did not help
i) weren't/were not
j) didn't/did not fly
k) didn't/did not give
l) didn't/did not travel

### Aufgabe 8

a) We were walking.
b) You were running.
c) I was jumping.
d) He was going.
e) They were turning.
f) She was stopping.
g) It was moving.

### Aufgabe 9

a) wasn't/was not walking; was walking
b) weren't/were not eating; were eating
c) were driving; weren't/were not driving
d) wasn't/was not wearing; was wearing
e) weren't/were not going; were going
f) weren't/were not telling; were telling
g) weren't/were not swimming; were swimming
h) weren't/were not flying; were flying
i) weren't/were not laughing; were crying

### Aufgabe 10

a) were chatting; left
b) told; arrived
c) was walking; went
d) were screaming; were
e) felt; was
f) took; was looking
g) was listening; asked
h) were having; was looking

### Aufgabe 11

(a) made
(b) was running
(c) came
(d) was crossing
(e) not watch
(f) didn't/did not see
(g) was riding
(h) stopped
(i) didn't/did not hurt
(j) was
(k) didn't/did not move
(l) didn't/did not bark
(m) was carrying
(n) put
(o) opened
(p) touched
(q) was
(r) was looking
(s) found
(t) fetched

## 5 Das *present perfect*

### Aufgabe 1

a) She has arrived.
b) He has left.
c) I have started.
d) You have stopped.
e) We have learned.
f) They have taught.
g) It has brought.
h) You have taken.

### Aufgabe 2

a) She hasn't/has not arrived.
b) He hasn't/has not left.
c) I haven't/have not started.
d) You haven't/have not stopped.
e) We haven't/have not learned.
f) They haven't/have not taught.
g) It hasn't/has not brought.
h) You haven't/have not taken.

### Aufgabe 3

a) has tidied; hasn't/has not tidied
b) have taken; haven't taken
c) has cleaned; hasn't/has not cleaned
d) has thrown; hasn't/has not thrown
e) have put; haven't put
f) has washed; hasn't/has not washed
g) have dusted; haven't dusted

### Aufgabe 4

a) has caught; has missed
b) has found; has lost
c) has won; has lost
d) has exchanged; has got
e) has scored; hasn't/has not kept

### Aufgabe 5

a) Tim has given Lily a bowl of milk.
b) Mrs Singasong has made her son a sandwich./Her son has made Mrs Singasong a sandwich.
c) Suzy has brought her father the newspaper./Her father has brought Suzy the newspaper.
d) Lily has carried a ball to Suzy./Suzy has carried a ball to Lily.
e) Mrs Singasong has shown her husband a pair of shoes./Her husband has shown Mrs Singasong a pair of shoes.

### Aufgabe 6

a) Have you ever been at the North Pole? – No, I have never been at the North Pole.
b) Have you ever slept in an igloo? – No, I have never slept in an igloo.
c) Have you ever spent a whole day in the dark? – No, I have never spent a whole day in the dark.
d) Have you ever eaten raw fish? – No, I have never eaten raw fish.
e) Have you ever ridden a dog sledge? – No, I have never ridden a dog sledge.
f) Have you ever walked on an iceberg? – No, I have never walked on an iceberg.

### Aufgabe 7

a) Have you already chosen a play? – No, I haven't chosen a play yet.
b) Have you already bought the theatre tickets? – No, I haven't bought the theatre tickets yet.
c) Have you already organized a bus? – No, I haven't organized a bus yet.
d) Have you already counted the pupils in our tutor group? – No, I haven't counted the pupils in our tutor group yet.
e) Have you already asked the headmaster for permission? – No, I haven't asked the headmaster for permission yet.
f) Have you already written a letter with information for the parents? – No, I haven't written a letter with information for the parents yet.
g) Have you already found any teachers who want to come with us? – No, I haven't found any teachers who want to come with us yet.

### Aufgabe 8

| | | | |
|---|---|---|---|
| (a) have been | (b) started | (c) was | (d) performed |
| (e) have had | (f) met | (g) have had | (h) thought |
| (i) told | (j) was | (k) have just had | (l) have decided |

### Aufgabe 9

a) Have you ever been
b) have travelled; went
c) Have you ever tried
d) ate; liked
e) Have you ever learned
f) had; have already forgotten
g) Have you already decided
h) haven't/have not talked; have just had

### Aufgabe 10

a) Last year we wrote a few English tests.
b) I have already done many exercises in this book.
c) I have never read so many English sentences.
d) This morning we had English at school.
e) I have just finished this exercise.

## 6 Zukunftsformen

### Aufgabe 1

a) You are going to begin the exercise.
b) I am going to write down a sentence.
c) He is going to explain the going to-future.
d) We are going to learn the rules.
e) They are going to choose the right form.
f) She is going to think of the answer.

### Aufgabe 2

a) Suzy is going to go the hairdresser. She isn't/is not going to buy a new T-shirt.
b) Tim is going to watch a volleyball match. He isn't/is not going to go to the cinema with Nat.
c) Mr and Mrs Singasong are going to play tennis. They aren't/are not going to have tea with their neighbours.
d) Tim is going to give a concert with the school orchestra. He isn't/is not going to work in the garden.
e) Mr and Mrs Singasong are going to buy vegetables at the market. They aren't/are not going to go swimming.

### Aufgabe 3

a) I will have lots of money. I will not/won't be poor.
b) You will own a big car. You will not/won't use the bus.
c) He will sell many CDs. He will not/won't be an unknown singer.
d) She will play in a film. She will not/won't do silly jobs.
e) We will travel a lot. We will not/won't stay at home.
f) They will have a lot of friends. They will not/won't feel lonely.

### Aufgabe 4

a) will wake b) will make c) will take d) will help
e) will go f) will buy

### Aufgabe 5

a) will not/won't wake b) will not/won't make
c) will not/won't take d) will not/won't help
e) will not/won't go f) will not/won't buy

### Aufgabe 6

a) are you going to do b) am going to give; won't be
c) Are you going to give d) will be; am going to work
e) will be f) will see; am not going to tell

### Aufgabe 7

a) will be b) am going to watch
c) are they going to come d) will come
e) Are you going to make f) I am going to bring
g) will make h) is going to be
i) am going to ask j) will say

## 7 Die modalen Hilfsverben

### Aufgabe 1

a) I can/I can't sing an English rap song.
b) I can/I can't bark like a dog.
c) I can/I can't write with my toes.
d) I can/I can't do a somersault.
e) I can/I can't walk on my hands.
f) I can/I can't spell my name backwards.
g) I can/I can't do a magic trick.
h) I can/I can't sleep a whole weekend.

### Aufgabe 2

a) He can/She can sing an English rap song./He can't/She can't …
b) He can/She can bark like a dog./He can't/She can't …
c) He can/She can write with his/her toes./He can't/She can't …
d) He can/She can do a somersault./He can't/She can't …
e) He can/She can walk on his/her hands./He can't/She can't …
f) He can/She can spell his/her name backwards./He can't/She can't …

g) He can/She can do a magic trick./He can't/She can't …
h) He can/She can sleep a whole weekend./He can't/She can't …

### Aufgabe 3

Can you switch on the light, please?
Can you repeat the phrase/these words, please?
Can you take out your books/your pens, please?
Can you close your books/the windows, please?
Can you clean the board/the classroom, please?
Can you write down the phrase/these words, please?
Can you tidy up your books/your pens/the classroom, please?
Can you open your books/the windows, please?

### Aufgabe 4

a) They must be polite to their parents.
b) They must tell their parents where they go.
c) They must come home before 8 pm.
d) They must do their homework every day.
e) They must talk about problems at school.
f) They must help with the housework once a day.
g) They must pay for their mobile phones with their pocket money.
h) They must introduce their friends to their parents.

### Aufgabe 5

a) They must not/mustn't read Tim's and Suzy's diaries.
b) They must not/mustn't control Tim's and Suzy's mails.
c) They must not/mustn't throw away any of Tim's and Suzy's clothes.
d) They must not/mustn't tidy up Tim's and Suzy's rooms.
e) They must not/mustn't look into Tim's and Suzy's school bags.
f) They must not/mustn't tell Tim and Suzy what to eat.
g) They must not/mustn't enter Tim's and Suzy's rooms without asking.
h) They must not/mustn't turn off Tim's and Suzy's music.

### Aufgabe 6

a) Tim and Suzy need not/needn't make the sandwiches for their school lunch.
b) Suzy need not/needn't mow the lawn.
c) Tim need not/needn't repair his bike.
d) Tim and Suzy need not/needn't iron their clothes.
e) Suzy need not/needn't bake tea cakes.
f) Tim and Suzy need not/needn't do the shopping.
g) Suzy need not/needn't wash the car.
h) Tim need not/needn't clean Lily's basket.

### Aufgabe 7

They needn't do the cooking.
They mustn't smoke.
They needn't wash the dishes.
They must pay the bill.
They can talk to the other guests.
They mustn't put their feet on the table.
They mustn't/needn't bring their own sandwiches.
They can/needn't order something to drink.

### Aufgabe 8

| | | | |
|---|---|---|---|
| a) needn't/need not | b) mustn't/must not | c) can | d) needn't/need not |
| e) can | f) mustn't/must not | g) must | h) needn't/need not |
| i) can | j) can't/cannot | | |

### Aufgabe 9

| | | | |
|---|---|---|---|
| a) Could | b) shall | c) May/Could | d) Could |
| e) shall | f) Could | g) Shall | h) May/Could |

### Aufgabe 10

Mögliche Lösungsfragen:

a) Could you turn on the heating in our room, please?
b) Could somebody repair the TV in our room, please?
c) May/could I get some ice-cream, please?
d) Could you change this twenty pound note for my mother, please?
e) Shall my father carry our bags to the hotel room?
f) Could my mother sit down on the sofa in the hotel lobby, please?

### Aufgabe 11

| | | | |
|---|---|---|---|
| a) Shall/~~Must~~ | b) can/~~mustn't~~ | c) must/~~needn't~~ | d) ~~Shall~~/May |
| e) must/~~could~~ | f) ~~mustn't~~/needn't | g) mustn't/~~must~~ | h) ~~shall~~/could |
| i) could/~~may~~ | j) ~~can~~/cannot; can/~~needn't~~ | | k) ~~must~~/can |
| l) ~~cannot~~/mustn't | | | |

# 8 Adjektive

## Aufgabe 1

a) happy; bad
b) warm; cold
c) right; wrong
d) full; empty
e) fast; slow
f) difficult; easy

## Aufgabe 2

a) I need longer jeans.
b) I need a smaller jumper.
c) I need a more interesting T-shirt.
d) I need cleaner shoes.
e) I need a shorter jacket.
f) I need bigger trousers.

## Aufgabe 3

a) highest
b) coldest
c) wettest
d) sunniest
e) deepest
f) most interesting
g) biggest
h) best
i) worst
j) most difficult

## Aufgabe 4

a) Lemonade is sweeter than mineral water. Mineral water is not as sweet as lemonade.
b) Apples are healthier than chocolate. Chocolate is not as healthy as apples.
c) A tomato is smaller than a pumpkin. A pumpkin is not as small as a tomato.
d) Coffee is bitterer than a banana milkshake. A banana milkshake is not as bitter as coffee.
e) Bread is drier than yoghurt. Yoghurt is not as dry as bread.
f) Chilies are hotter than carrots. Carrots are not as hot as chilies.
g) A muffin is softer than a nut. A nut is not as soft as a muffin.

## Aufgabe 5

a) "Crazy Love" is not as sad as "Vampire Nights".
But it is sadder than "Guns and Horses".
b) "Vampire Nights" is not as romantic as "Crazy Love".
But it is more romantic than "Guns and Horses".
c) "Guns and Horses" is not as short as "Crazy Love".
But it is shorter than "Vampire Nights".
d) "Guns and Horses" is not as exciting as "Vampire Nights".
But it is more exciting than "Crazy Love".
e) "Guns and Horses" is not as scary as "Vampire Nights".
But it is scarier than "Crazy Love".
f) "Crazy Love" is not as funny as "Guns and Horses".
But it is funnier than "Vampire Nights".

g) "Guns and Horses" is not as boring as "Crazy Love".
But it is more boring than "Vampire Nights".

Hier sind natürlich auch andere Sätze möglich. Entscheidend ist jeweils die richtige grammatikalische Konstruktion!

**Aufgabe 6**

| | | | |
|---|---|---|---|
| a) much homework | b) many pupils | c) many books | d) many pencils |
| e) many exercises | f) much grammar | g) many tables | h) many bags |
| i) much paper | j) many tests | k) many questions | l) much information |

**Aufgabe 7**

| | | | |
|---|---|---|---|
| a) a few eggs | b) a little butter | c) a little sugar | d) a little flour |
| e) a little milk | f) a few raisins | g) a little chocolate | h) a few nuts |

**Aufgabe 8**

| | |
|---|---|
| a) ~~much~~/many | b) ~~a little~~/a few; a lot of/~~a little~~ |
| c) ~~much~~/many | d) a few/~~a little~~; ~~many~~/a lot of |
| e) much/~~many~~ | f) much/~~many~~; ~~a few~~/a little |
| g) ~~much~~/many | h) ~~a little~~/a few; much/~~many~~ |

# 9 Adverbien

## Aufgabe 1

| | |
|---|---|
| a) quietly; loudly | b) well; badly |
| c) carefully; terribly | d) slowly; quickly |
| e) excitingly; boringly | |

## Aufgabe 2

| | |
|---|---|
| a) happy | happily |
| b) easy | easily |
| c) angry | angrily |
| d) friendly | in a friendly way |
| e) hungry | hungrily |
| f) funny | funnily |

## Aufgabe 3

a) Mr Singasong cooks well.
b) Mrs Singasong drives carefully.
c) Tim sings fantastically.
d) Suzy dances beautifully.
e) Mrs Singasong plays badminton aggressively.
f) Tim swims fast.
g) Suzy speaks nervously.
h) Mr Singasong paints awfully.
i) Tim works hard.
j) Mrs Singasong acts nicely.

## Aufgabe 4

| | | | |
|---|---|---|---|
| a) excited | b) terrible | c) good | d) loudly |
| e) spookily | f) scary | g) hard | h) angrily |
| i) carefully | j) nicely | k) special | l) brilliant |

## Aufgabe 5

a) A horse can run fast, but I can run faster.
b) A bird can sing beautifully, but I can sing more beautifully.
c) A duck can swim well, but I can swim better.
d) A fox can act cleverly, but I can act more cleverly.
e) A mouse can move quietly, but I can move more quietly.
f) A bull can fight aggressively, but I can fight more aggressively.
g) A cow can eat slowly, but I can eat more slowly.
h) A snake can dance elegantly, but I can dance more elegantly.

i) A dog can bark angrily, but I can bark more angrily.
j) A bee can work hard, but I can work harder.

### Aufgabe 6

Mögliche Lösungen:

a) I can run faster than a horse, but I can't run as fast as a racing car.
b) I can sing more beautifully than a bird, but I can't sing as beautifully as an opera singer.
c) I can swim better than a duck, but I can't swim as well as a fish.
d) I can act more cleverly than a fox, but I can't act as cleverly as my older sister.
e) I can move more quietly than a mouse, but I can't move as quietly as a ghost.
f) I can fight more aggressively than a bull, but I can't fight as aggressively as a tiger.
g) I can eat more slowly than a cow, but I can't eat as slowly as a sheep.
h) I can dance more elegantly than a snake, but I can't dance as elegantly as a ballet dancer.
i) I can bark more angrily than a dog, but I can't bark as angrily as a wolf.
j) I can work harder than a bee, but I can't work as hard as our caretaker.

### Aufgabe 7

a) David runs quickly, Stefan runs more quickly and Paolo runs most quickly.
b) Stefan moves elegantly, David moves more elegantly and Paolo moves most elegantly.
c) Paolo plays fairly, Stefan plays more fairly and David plays most fairly.
d) David kicks hard, Paolo kicks harder and Stefan kicks hardest.
e) Stefan performs tricks well, Paolo performs tricks better and David performs tricks best.
f) Paolo eats healthily, David eats more healthily and Stefan eats most healthily.
g) Paolo acts badly, Stefan acts worse and David acts worst.
h) Stefan celebrates a goal happily, David celebrates a goal more happily and Paolo celebrates a goal most happily.
i) David talks interestingly, Paolo talks more interestingly and Stefan talks most interestingly.
j) Stefan smiles nicely, David smiles more nicely and Paolo smiles most nicely.

### Aufgabe 8

a) Stefan doesn't run as quickly as Paolo, but he runs more quickly than David.
b) David doesn't move as elegantly as Paolo, but he moves more elegantly than Stefan.
c) Stefan doesn't play as fairly as David, but he plays more fairly than Paolo.
d) Paolo doesn't kick as hard as Stefan, but he kicks harder than David.
e) Paolo doesn't perform tricks as well as David, but he performs tricks better than Stefan.
f) David doesn't eat as healthily as Stefan, but he eats more healthily than Paolo.
g) Stefan doesn't act as badly as David, but he acts worse than Paolo.
h) David doesn't celebrate a goal as happily as Paolo, but he celebrates a goal more happily than Stefan.
i) Paolo doesn't talk as interestingly as Stefan, but he talks more interestingly than David.
j) David doesn't smile as nicely as Paolo, but he smiles more nicely than Stefan.

# 10 Fragen

## Aufgabe 1

a) Do you touch snakes and spiders?
b) Do you swim in ice-cold water?
c) Do you go outside during a thunderstorm?
d) Do you walk into a dark forest at night?
e) Do you climb steep rocks?
f) Do you dream of a bungee-jump?
g) Do you like roller-coaster rides?
h) Do you eat flies and worms?

Die Kurzantwort lautet jeweils: Yes, I do./No, I don't.

Für jedes Ja erhältst du 1 Punkt, für jedes Nein 0 Punkte.

| | |
|---|---|
| 0–3 Punkte: | You really hate adventures. |
| 4–8 Punkte: | A few adventures are fine for you. |
| 9–10 Punkte: | You are a real adventurer. You are ready for the jungle! |

## Aufgabe 2

a) Is Berlin the capital of the USA? No, it isn't.
b) Are mice the biggest animals on earth? No, they aren't.
c) Can you visit many sights in New York? Yes, you can.
d) Has Germany got a king? No, it hasn't.
e) Do polar bears live in Africa? No, they don't.
f) Does the River Thames run through London? Yes, it does.
g) Have the English got many kinds of tea? Yes, they have.
h) Can penguins fly? No, they can't.

## Aufgabe 3

a) Is Luke writing a test? No, he isn't.
b) Is Megan asking a question? No, she isn't.
c) Are Josh and Harry listening to the teacher? No, they aren't.
d) Is Sophie doing maths? No, she isn't.

## Aufgabe 4

a) Did Suzy and Tim play a trick on their father on the $1^{st}$ of April? Yes, they did.
b) Did Mr Singasong laugh about Suzy's question? Yes, he did.
c) Did Tim look shocked when he saw his father? Yes, he did.
d) Did Mr Singasong hurry back into the bathroom to look into the mirror? Yes, he did.
e) Did Suzy and Tim run away after their trick? Yes, they did.
f) Did Mr Singasong go to work as a punk? No, he didn't.

### Aufgabe 5

a) Was Tim eating crisps? Yes, he was.
b) Was Suzy drinking coke? Yes, she was.
c) Was Mr Singasong reading the newspaper? No, he wasn't.
d) Was Mrs Singasong doing a crossword puzzle? Yes, she was.
e) Was Lily sitting on the sofa? Yes, she was.
f) Were Tim and Suzy having a fight? No, they weren't.
g) Was Mrs Singasong phoning her mother? No, she wasn't.
h) Was Mr Singasong blowing his horn? No, he wasn't.

### Aufgabe 6

a) Have you ever bought the wrong present for your best friend's birthday?
b) Have you ever told a lie to your best friend?
c) Have you ever stolen anything from your best friend?
d) Have you ever talked badly about your best friend?
e) Have you ever been jealous of your best friend?
f) Have you ever hidden a secret from your best friend?
g) Have you ever kissed your best friend's boyfriend/girlfriend?
h) Have you ever forgotten to call your best friend?

Die Kurzantwort lautet jeweils: Yes, I have./No, I haven't.

Für jedes Ja erhältst du 1 Punkt, für jedes Nein 0 Punkte.

Gesamtauswertung:

| | |
|---|---|
| 0 Punkte: | You are a true best friend. |
| 1–4 Punkte: | You do not always act (*verhalten*) like a best friend. |
| 5–8 Punkte: | You do a lot of things a best friend shouldn't do. |

### Aufgabe 7

a) Is Lily going to go drink some milk? Yes, she is.
Is she going to eat a mouse? No, she isn't.
b) Is Lily going to get some sleep? Yes, she is.
Is she going to go for a walk? No, she isn't.
c) Is Lily going to play with her ball? Yes, she is.
Is she going to stay in her basket? No, she isn't.
d) Is Lily going to fight with Tim? Yes, she is.
Is Lily going to sleep again? No, she isn't.

### Aufgabe 8

a) Will all people speak Chinese? Yes, they will./No, they won't.
b) Will robots serve breakfast? Yes, they will./No, they won't.
c) Will tourists spend their holidays on Mars? Yes, they will./No, they won't.
d) Will all houses be skyscrapers? Yes, they will./No, they won't.
e) Will cars fly from one place to another? Yes, they will./No, they won't.
f) Will we see palm-trees at the North Pole? Yes, we will./No, we won't.
g) Will we buy everything in online shops? Yes, we will./No, we won't.

### Aufgabe 9

a) How do I get to London Zoo?
b) What is the way to the next bus station?
c) Where can I buy a bottle of water?
d) What can I do at the British Museum?
e) How much must I pay for a tube ticket?
f) When is the next guided tour at the Tower?
g) Why are British policemen called Bobbies?
h) Who can I see at Buckingham Palace?
i) When does the London Dungeon close?
j) Where can I find Sherlock Holmes's house?

### Aufgabe 10

a) Where is this woman reading a book?
b) What is that woman drinking?
c) What is this man buying?
d) Why is that man laughing?
e) Where are these girls going?
f) Where are those girls lying?
g) How are these boys going to the concert?
h) What are those boys wearing?
i) Where are these people waiting?
j) Who are those people watching?

## Aufgabe 11

a) How did you become an actor?
b) When did you start acting?
c) What did you do to get famous?
d) Where did you play your first role?
e) How did you learn about your talent?
f) Why were you in Hollywood last month?
g) When did you hear about your Academy Award?
h) How did your mother react to your prize?
i) What did your wife say about your prize?
j) Where did you go after the Academy Awards party?

## Aufgabe 12

a) What was your wife wearing at the party?
b) Who was sitting at your table with you?
c) What were you having for dinner?
d) Why were you laughing so much?
e) What were you talking about during dinner?
f) What were you telling your film partners?
g) Why was your wife looking so angry?
h) Where were your five big dogs during the party?

## Aufgabe 13

a) Where has Mr Singasong broken a cup?
b) Why has Tim slipped?
c) Where has Mrs Singasong lost an earring?
d) What has Suzy left at home?
e) What haven't Mr and Mrs Singasong remembered?
f) Where has Mrs Singasong thrown an important letter?
g) What has Mr Singasong put on?
h) Where has Tim left his house keys?
i) Why hasn't Mrs Singasong's car started?
j) What has Suzy used for her tea?

### Aufgabe 14

a) What are you going to do in your holidays?
b) When are you going to go to bed tonight?
c) Where are you going to spend your weekend?
d) Why are you going to use the internet?
e) Who are you going to meet at school?
f) When are you going to do your homework?
g) What are you going to tell your friend?
h) When are you going to practise your English again?

### Aufgabe 15

a) What will my future be like?
b) Where/How will I live?
c) When/Where/How will I finish school?
d) When will I have children?
e) Where/What will I work?
f) What will I do as a job?
g) Where/When/How will I find a partner?

### Aufgabe 16

a) What does Tim always use?
b) Where is Suzy hiding Tim's hair gel?
c) What is Tim going to put into his sister's bed?
d) When did Mrs Singasong take Suzy's mobile phone without asking her?
e) Why was Suzy using her mother's phone for a three hours' call?
f) What must Suzy pay with her pocket money?
g) What has Mr Singasong done?
h) What is Mrs Singasong drinking now?
i) How will everybody feel in the end?

### Aufgabe 17

a) Who has seen this cat?
b) Who knows anything about its owner?
c) Who feeds the cat normally?
d) What is the name of the cat?
e) What makes the cat angry?
f) Who opened our kitchen window last night?
g) What happened in our kitchen at night?

### Aufgabe 18

a) Who was in the Singasongs' kitchen at night?
b) What did she hear in the garden?
c) Who did she see at the kitchen window?
d) What was open?
e) Who climbed through the window into the kitchen?
f) What did he want?
g) Who drank Lily's milk?
h) Who didn't feel happy about that?

### Aufgabe 19

a) Why have you called me?
b) What is your problem?
c) When did the cat come to your house?
d) Who found the cat?
e) Where was it?
f) What was the strange cat drinking?
g) How has the cat acted since then?
h) Who has broken all those milk bottles over there?
i) What (else) has it destroyed?
j) What makes the cat calm?
k) Why don't you want to keep the cat?

### Aufgabe 20

| | | | |
|---|---|---|---|
| a) didn't you? | b) isn't she? | c) hasn't she? | d) don't you? |
| e) won't you? | f) doesn't she? | g) can't she? | h) can she? |
| i) has she? | j) does she? | k) is she? | l) will you? |
| m) am I? | | | |

### Aufgabe 21

| | | | |
|---|---|---|---|
| a) aren't you? | b) has he? | c) isn't he? | d) won't he? |
| e) hasn't he? | f) did he? | g) does he? | h) will you? |

### Aufgabe 22

a) We didn't/did not get any homework, did we?
b) We will write an English test next week, won't we?
c) We go to assembly every Monday morning, don't we?
d) The school band hasn't/has not met yet, has it?

# 11 Satzstruktur und Wortstellung

## Aufgabe 1

a) At 6.30 am my alarm clock rings.
My alarm clock rings at 6.30.

b) Ten minutes later I get up.
I get up ten minutes later.

c) Every Monday I feel especially tired.
I feel especially tired every Monday.

d) But every Sunday morning I feel very happy.
But I feel very happy every Sunday morning.

e) Every weekend I stay in bed as long as I like.
I stay in bed as long as I like every weekend.

## Aufgabe 2

a) I watch TV in the living-room.
b) I brush my teeth in the bathroom.
c) I read books in my bedroom.
d) I have breakfast in the kitchen.
e) I put my clothes in the hall.

## Aufgabe 3

a) Every day I practise the piano at school./I practise the piano at school every day.
b) Twice a week I play tennis at my tennis club./I play tennis at my tennis club twice a week.
c) Every Wednesday I take dancing lessons in town./I take dancing lessons in town every Wednesday.
d) Every Friday I do taekwondo at the gym./I do taekwondo at the gym every Friday.
e) On Sundays I play football on the sports ground./I play football on the sports ground on Sundays.

## Aufgabe 4

a) Sometimes Tim can eat a lot of chocolate. / Tim can sometimes eat a a lot of chocolate.
b) But he never feels sick after that.
c) Suzy never watches action films alone.
d) But sometimes she must watch them with Tim. / But she must sometimes watch them with Tim.
e) Sometimes Suzy and Tim have trouble with each other. / Suzy and Tim sometimes have trouble with each other.
f) But they never tell their parents about it.

### Aufgabe 5

a) He is always polite. But she doesn't always answer in a friendly way.
b) They must always do their homework. They must always show it to the teacher.
c) We were always happy as children. We always spent a lot of time outdoors.
d) They have always lived in this house. They have always liked it here a lot.
e) You will always be my best friend. I will always be there for you.

### Aufgabe 6

a) Lily can't sing beautifully. She cries terribly at night in the Singasongs' house.
b) Suzy plays the saxophone fantastically. But she whistles awfully from time to time.
c) Suzy's mum rides the bike badly. But she drives her taxi well every day.
d) Tim walks slowly to school./Tim walks to school slowly. But he runs home fast in the evening.

### Aufgabe 7

a) If she wins, she will be a millionaire.
b) If she is a millionaire, she will stop working.
c) If she stops working, she will have lots of free time.
d) If she has lots of free time, she will travel to other countries.
e) If she travels to other countries, she won't see her family much.
f) If she doesn't see her family much, she won't be happy.
g) If she isn't happy, she won't care about all the money.

### Aufgabe 8

a) If I win, I will have lots of money.
b) If I have lots of money, I will go shopping every day.
c) If I go shopping every day, I won't have time for my homework.
d) If I don't have time for my homework, I will get into trouble.

### Aufgabe 9

a) If you are cold, close the window./If you are cold, go for a long run.
b) If you are hungry, make yourself a sandwich.
c) If you are nervous, do some yoga exercises./If you are nervous, talk about it to a friend./If you are nervous, go for a long run.
d) If you are tired, get some sleep./If you are tired, do some yoga exercises.
e) If you are thirsty, drink a glass of water.
f) If you are sad, talk about it to a friend.
g) If you are angry, go for a long run./If you are angry, talk about it to a friend./If you are angry, do some yoga exercises.

## Aufgabe 10

Mögliche Sätze (es sind jeweils auch andere Modalverben und Kombinationen denkbar):

a) If you go to Madame Tussaud's, you can see Michael Jackson in wax.
b) If you stay for a week, you should buy a one-week tube ticket.
c) If you are interested in theatre, you must watch a play at the Globe Theatre.
d) If you want to do some shopping, you should try the shops on Oxford Street.
e) If you visit Buckingham Palace, you can take a look at the guards.
f) If you enjoy parks, you should make a picnic in Hyde Park.
g) If you like old things, you must go to Portobello Market.

## Aufgabe 11

| | | | |
|---|---|---|---|
| a) If | b) if | c) When | d) If |
| e) If | f) when | g) When | h) If |
| i) When | j) If | | |

## Aufgabe 12

| | | | |
|---|---|---|---|
| (a) who | (b) which | (c) who | (d) which |
| (e) which | (f) who | (g) which | (h) who |
| (i) which | (j) which | | |

## Aufgabe 13

a) The girl who/that is sitting next to me is called Olivia.
b) The jacket which/that has black stripes on it is hers.
c) The boy who/that has got red hair is called George.
d) The blue pen which/that he always uses was my present.
e) The girl whose name is Sophie lives in my street.
f) She has a skateboard which/that she rides every day.
g) The boy whose name is Daniel is a good friend of mine.
h) The shoes whose colour is black look very smart.
i) The girl who/that plays football is called Lisa.
j) She often wears a T-shirt which/that she got from a famous football player.

**Aufgabe 14**

a) The exercises which/that you can find in this book are all about grammar./The exercises you can find in this book are all about grammar.
b) Maybe it has helped you with some of the problems which/that you have had with grammar./Maybe it has helped you with some of the problems you have had with grammar.
c) The exercises which/that are easy can be done quickly.
d) Exercises which/that you must work on longer are more difficult./Exercises you must work on longer are more difficult.
e) The pupils who/that have done all the exercises have done a very good job.

## Verzeichnis grammatischer Fachausdrücke

| Englischer Begriff | Übersetzung | Beispiel |
|---|---|---|
| adjective | Adjektiv (Eigenschaftswort) | old |
| adverb<br>- of frequency<br>- of manner | Adverb (Umstandswort)<br>- der Häufigkeit<br>- der Art und Weise | <br>sometimes<br>quickly |
| adverbial | adverbiale Bestimmung (Satzbestimmung) | I meet her at 7 o'clock. |
| comparative | Komparativ (1. Steigerungsform des Adjektivs/Adverbs) | older |
| consonant | Konsonant (Mitlaut) | b, t, g |
| defining relative clause | notwendiger Relativsatz | The boy who is sitting next to me is my friend. |
| definite article | bestimmter Artikel (bestimmter Begleiter) | the house |
| demonstrative determiner | Demonstrativbegleiter (hinweisender Begleiter) | this girl |
| demonstrative pronoun | Demonstrativpronomen (hinweisendes Fürwort) | This is Tim. |
| future<br>- going to-future<br>- will-future | Futur (Zukunft) | <br>He is going to win.<br>She will be 18 soon. |
| genitive<br>- *s*-genitive<br>- *of*-genitive | Genitiv (2. Fall) | <br>the girl's bag<br>the door of the car |

| Englischer Begriff | Übersetzung | Beispiel |
|---|---|---|
| if-clause | Bedingungssatz | If she doesn't come … |
| imperative | Imperativ (Befehlsform) | Get up! |
| indefinite article | unbestimmter Artikel | a table |
| indefinite pronoun | Indefinitpronomen (unbestimmtes Fürwort) | some cake |
| infinitive | Infinitiv (Grundform) | (to) do |
| irregular | unregelmäßig | |
| modal (verb) | Modalverb, modales Hilfsverb | can, must, should |
| noun | Nomen, Substantiv (Hauptwort) | chair |
| object | Objekt (Satzergänzung) | I can see the sun. |
| past participle | Partizip II, Partizip Perfekt (Mittelwort der Vergangenheit) | talked, taken |
| past progressive | Verlaufsform des *past tense* | She was singing. |
| past tense | 1. Vergangenheit | I smiled.<br>I was smiling. |
| personal pronoun | Personalpronomen (persönliches Fürwort) | you |
| plural | Plural (Mehrzahl) | two apples |
| possessive determiner | Possessivbegleiter (besitzanzeigender Begleiter) | my pen |

## Verzeichnis grammatischer Fachausdrücke

| Englischer Begriff | Übersetzung | Beispiel |
|---|---|---|
| possessive pronoun | Possessivpronomen (besitzanzeigendes Fürwort) | It is mine. |
| predicate | Prädikat (Satzaussage) | I like tea. |
| present perfect | 2. Vergangenheit | He has gone. |
| present *progress*ive | Verlaufsform des present tense | They are laughing. |
| present tense | Präsens (Gegenwart) | He walks.<br>He is walking. |
| question tag | Bestätigungsfrage | It's nice, isn't it? |
| regular | regelmäßig | |
| relative pronoun | Relativpronomen | The man who has big feet needs big shoes. |
| *simple* past | einfache Form des past tense | You swam. |
| simple present | einfache Form des *present tense* | I write. |
| singular | Singular (Einzahl) | (a) tree |
| subject | Subjekt (Satzgegenstand) | Suzy goes to school. |
| superlative | Superlativ (2. Steigerungsform des Adjektivs/Adverbs) | the oldest |
| verb | Verb (Zeitwort/Tunwort) | to play |

## Quellennachweis

**Bildnachweis:**
Zeichnungen: Katja Rau, Berglen: 9, 11, 15, 17, 18, 34, 39, 53, 81, 109, 125;
Shutterstock, New York: 31 (Rvector)

Der Verlag hat sich nach bestem Wissen und Gewissen bemüht, alle Inhaber von Urheberrechten an Texten und Abbildungen zu diesem Werk ausfindig zu machen. Sollte das in irgendeinem Fall nicht korrekt geschehen sein, bitten wir um Entschuldigung und bieten an, gegebenenfalls in einer nachfolgenden Auflage einen korrigierten Quellennachweis zu bringen.